CW00903893

THE MOBIUS GUIDES
star signs

THE MOBIUS GUIDES

star signs

KRISTYNA ARCARTI

HODDER
MOBIUS

Copyright © 1999, 2003 by Kristyna Arcarti

First published in Great Britain in 2003 by Hodder and Stoughton
A division of Hodder Headline

The right of Kristyna Arcarti to be identified as the Author
of the Work has been asserted by her in accordance with the
Copyright, Designs and Patents Act 1988.

A Mobius paperback

10 9 8 7 6 5 4 3 2 1

All rights reserved. No part of this publication may be reproduced, stored
in a retrieval system, or transmitted, in any form or by any means without
the prior written permission of the publisher, nor be otherwise circulated
in any form of binding or cover other than that in which it is published
and without a similar condition being imposed on the subsequent
purchaser.

A CIP catalogue record for this title is
available from the British Library

ISBN 0 34073476 0

Typeset in Fairfield Light by
Palimpsest Book Production Limited, Polmont, Stirlingshire
Printed and bound in Great Britain by Mackays of Chatham plc,
Chatham, Kent

Hodder and Stoughton
A division of Hodder Headline
338 Euston Road
London NW1 3BH

contents

introduction

Many people think of star signs merely in terms of what the stars tell them for the day; there is, however, much more to astrology than this narrow application of the science. This book aims to correct some misconceptions about star signs, give easily understood information and enable you, the reader, to find out a little more about yourself and those around you.

It is very easy, of course, to stereotype people, but everyone is an individual, and often people from the same star sign will differ widely. The reasons for this are many and varied, but the reason often overlooked by those who wish to devalue the science of astrology is that a person's character is shaped not only by their star sign, but the position of each of the planets at the time of their birth and also the ascending or rising sign. So often people will remark that two people with the same birthday are quite different and go on to reject astrology as a result. The aims of this book are to show the major characteristics of each sign, giving both positive and negative traits, and to point people in the right direction with regard to jobs, relationships and likely health problems, while emphasising that everyone is ultimately in charge of their own destiny. Free will is something that can override any planetary aspects.

Years ago, mainly for amusement, I set to work to look at all the people around me. I found out their birthdates, and without their knowledge, drew up charts to see how they related to me, or did not, as the case might be. The results were very interesting, and in a couple of cases quite revealing!

Without having a detailed knowledge of star signs or knowing how to draw up a natal chart, you may not get the full benefits from this sort of exercise, but even by finding out someone's birth sign, you can have a great deal of fun working out who will get on with who and identifying star sign traits.

Compatibilities are something we will deal with later on, but even with limited information covering only the star sign, you may find you receive insights which are helpful in both working and personal relationships. You may also learn why your Aries mother reacts to a situation in one way, whereas a Taurean mother would react in another; whether you yourself would make a good parent; and whether you were the ideal child!

If you are thinking about a change of direction in your career, or you are about to leave school and are wondering which way to go, astrology can help by giving an indication of the type or types of work for which you would be best suited.

Above all, this book is aimed to provide enjoyment and fun; it would be a great bonus if it also sparked within you the desire to learn more about the ancient art of astrology.

Astrological dates

Different astrologers often use different dates for the start and end of a zodiac sign, and this can be confusing, especially for the beginner, so we'll look at this briefly now.

Let's take the example of *Sagittarius*. Some astrologers maintain that this sign commences on 23 November. I would agree with this; other astrologers, however, suggest that

Sagittarius commences on 22 November. Maybe you don't think that this is much of a difference, but one day makes a lot of difference if you were born on 22 November – would you be a Sagittarius, or would you be a Scorpio?

The rule to remember, should you be born on the date of the commencement of a sign (whichever date that is) or on the date when a sign ends, is that you will be affected by *both* star signs. Such people are called *cusps*; in fact, it is generally accepted that the three or four days into a sign and the three or four days at the end of the sign are cusp cases, and that people born during that period will have characteristics of both signs.

aries

Aries, 21 March – 20 April
Aries – The first sign of the zodiac, and a fire sign, ruled by Mars. The sign for Aries represents the ram and its horns.

Rams are by their very nature leaders of their flock, and Aries is very much a leader. As the sign is ruled by the planet Mars, Arians are naturally active people. Mars also gives aggression and single-mindedness and Arians will naturally want to be leaders in their chosen field.

Characteristics

Aries people are often strong, both physically and emotionally, and go through life with an enthusiasm seldom seen amongst the other signs. Not content with looking back at the past, they strive on into the future, knowing what they want, where they want to end up, and ultimately planning the way to get there.

Very much like the diamond, their chosen birthstone, they seem hard, but they can chip and crack. Arians by nature put themselves before others, but they are not selfish – it just does not occur to them to do otherwise. They are very loving, especially towards children and animals, and protective of those close to them. Aries people also like to touch – you will see them touching others, touching fabrics in shops, touching most things; they are very tactile. Arians are quick minded, and great company to be with. They are imaginative, enthusiastic and often the life and soul of the party; they have a great sense of fun, and will enjoy doing the most outlandish things, provided they know that nothing and no-one will be hurt by their actions.

Fashion

Aries people seldom think of buying clothes to last, but go for bright, happy outfits which will create a visual impact. Red is a favourite colour and trousers are popular with female Rams.

Money Matters

Aries people like challenge, and often deliberately look for jobs and relationships which are challenging to them. However, although they often enjoy the start of a project or job they quickly become bored by detail and routine. They have a desire for money, as well as for authority and power; often it is a tussle to see which of these two win through.

The money the Aries person earns is likely to be carefully guarded. Although Aries people love a gamble and like taking risks, from betting on slot machines and horses through to the Stock Market, and will splash money out on clothes and status symbols quite happily, ask them to part with money as a loan or gift, and they suddenly become quite tight-fisted and mean.

When buying items for the house, they will only buy what they want. If they live alone, they are likely to buy only enough food for the next meal, scouring supermarkets for items which have been reduced because they are close to their sell-by date or for produce which is slightly damaged and therefore reduced.

Improvements Needed

Whatever their age, Arians seldom acknowledge their true age, thinking themselves forever young. Sometimes this is a problem and they may need to look more carefully at themselves and the appropriateness of their behaviour at times.

They should try to pay more attention to detail; they tend to rush at things and should take more time. They should learn to be more patient, exercise more self-control and curb their tendency to frustration when things do not go as planned or expected.

In The Home

Space in a home is important to the Arian; they like to have room to spread themselves about. Very stylish and individual in their taste, they like homes which are showy and bold.

Although they are unlikely to be very keen on gardening, they have green fingers and like things which grow quickly. Similarly impatient in the kitchen, they have little time for meals which require much preparation or planning.

They love gadgets, and their homes are often cluttered with the latest kitchen aids, some of which never get used and stay in drawers gathering dust. Arians also love travel, especially fast travel, and hate delays. They love anything that provides excitement and even female Arians may have an interest in motor racing. Good at sports and games which combine skill and chance, they make excellent card players, and will also regard any fitness training as a competition.

Partnerships

Arians take love very seriously and are quite vulnerable, despite their apparently hard exterior. Arians are naturally flirtatious, and the female of the sign may have problems with men who take their friendliness as a sign of something more serious. Arians often have a quick affair for the fun and excitement of it rather than for anything more permanent. Arians in love are all or nothing people, sentimental, romantic and impulsive.

Aries people will find themselves naturally drawn to other fire signs (Leo and Sagittarius). Aries may be the most sexually demanding sign in the zodiac and most Arians have a very strong sex-drive. It is therefore essential for them to find a partner with similar needs, as otherwise problems can result. Often an Aries person will marry without thinking things through, and consequently a bad match can result.

If thinking in terms of a permanent relationship or marriage, Arian males should look towards Taureans or Capricornians (both earth signs) for a long-lasting match, Arians, Leos, Virgoans, Sagittarians and Pisceans for a particularly emotional match, Cancerians for a romantic match and Librans for a happy match. Those to avoid, if at all possible, are Geminians, Scorpios and Aquarians.

Female Arians looking at marriage should also think of avoiding Aquarians, Geminians and Scorpios, looking more at Taureans and Virgoans for stability, Cancerians, Librans and Pisceans for romance, Leos and Arians for passion and Sagittarians and Capricornians for a long-lasting marriage.

It is worth bearing in mind, whatever sex, that two Arians together may find their similarities and passions disruptive.

Arians as Parents

With their natural love of independence and challenge, the Arian parent will encourage their children to be themselves and take as many risks as they want to.

Sometimes the natural tactlessness and short temper of the Arian parent will upset a child, and Arian parents prefer to have strong children with strong wills, rather than children who want to stay peacefully at home.

The Aries father is a fun father, someone who will want to join in play activities, sports or adventures (but who will want to end up winning any races or games).

Arian mothers are warm but demand a tidy house, and problems will result if children are not as tidy as the Arian mother would wish. Sometimes the Arian mother will be impulsive, and to a child who is happy doing things on the spur of the moment, the Arian mother will be great fun; however, to a child who prefers routine and structure, the Arian mother's impulsiveness will be a strain.

Arian parents will get on very well with children born under the signs of Aries, Leo, Libra and Sagittarius, fairly well with children born under the sign of Gemini, tolerably well with Taurus, Cancer, Scorpio, Capricorn and Pisces, but there may be problems with a child born under the sign of Virgo.

Arians as Siblings

If you have a brother or sister who is an Arian, you will most definitely know they are around. They will be fun to be with and certainly very active, and if you feel you can keep up with them, will be good friends and very supportive in any arguments. If there is trouble, and they come off worse, they will try to keep their upset to themselves, preferring to be alone with their tears rather than show they are upset.

There can be quite a lot of rivalry with Arian siblings, and they may do all they can to come out on top of any arguments. However, Arians don't hold grudges or resentments once arguments or disagreements are over, and in turn, they will find it difficult to understand anyone who harbours resentment for their own past actions.

As they get older, the Arian brother or sister will continue to tell you everything they are doing, basically in the hope that they are doing better than you; it is all innocently meant, but being on top, and, as a result, being respected, matters greatly to Arians.

Arians as Friends

Whether the friendship is platonic or not, Arians are good friends.

In a living together relationship, Arians will get on with most other zodiac signs, but a fellow Arian or a Scorpio could present problems.

In a purely friendship relationship, Arians will have a fun friendship with Geminians and Sagittarians, a difficult friendship with Arians, Taureans, Virgoans and Capricornians, a very strong friendship with Librans, Leos (provided the other person doesn't decide to compete) Scorpios and Aquarians, and reasonably well with the remaining signs.

Arians at Work

If you work with an Aries person, you will definitely know it! Arians are good bosses, but can be demanding. They expect everything to be done in a professional way, because that is how they themselves do things. They react well under pressure, and often this gives them the opportunity to really shine. However, if their colleagues don't cope well they may bear the brunt of one of Aries' verbal attacks.

It will sometimes be difficult to understand an Arian boss, as when least expected, they will want to sit and chat. Sometimes Arians will seem totally disorganised; if working for an Aries boss, be prepared to have to sift through piles of papers on their desk to find what you are looking for. Although Arians will claim to know exactly where everything is and to have a system, it will be totally incomprehensible to most fellow-workers.

Those Arians who haven't yet made it to the top will never give up trying. They will work long and hard to make the correct impression, and will often succeed.

Arians love a challenge, and the sort of jobs they are best suited for must encompass this. Anything which also involves an element of risk every now and again is also good for them. Not particularly interested in detail, they are often better at a project's inception rather than managing it through to completion. They are best suited for a job which moves quickly, is energetic, and gives them opportunities for decision making.

Appropriate jobs would include the army or allied services, politics, sport, sales, finance, lecturing, exploration, company management, or medicine. It is possible that Arians will find themselves working for environmental or humanitarian causes, as they will enjoy the challenge and the feeling of being a pioneer, while contributing to their surroundings and to humanity as a whole. Many Arians will be their own boss and are ideally suited to having their own business, as they are not afraid of hard work and are willing to put an enormous amount of time and effort into any new enterprise.

Arians and Health

Naturally active, few Arians suffer from weight problems; their energy and activity levels keep the pounds at bay. They may however, suffer from headaches or migraines, due to their gruelling work schedules, which sometimes make them carry on working long after their body tells them to stop. At times such as these, Arians may, due to their speed of action and eventual tiredness, become liable to minor, clumsy accidents; they should learn to slow down a little and stop before they reach this stage. Mars, their ruling planet, urges action, drive and daring, and often this will cause problems. Aries people should learn to listen to their bodies a little more and rest when signs indicate this would be best.

The Arians' tendency to work through lunchbreaks and eat the wrong sorts of foods can sometimes lead to nutritional imbalances, and they should pay attention to the vitamin and mineral content of foods. They should also try to eat regular meals, and eat them sitting down rather than on the hoof. Arians should try to control toxins in the system to reduce the cases of kidney problems common to the star sign.

Upset stomachs can also be a problem, due to the Arians' quick tempers, which upset their systems and then lead on to migraines. All Arians should learn the art of relaxation, as stress can take its toll when things aren't going well or emotions are bottled up.

The need for challenge in Arians could lead many to taking up challenging, risky sports to keep fit, and many will look to tennis, fencing or a martial art, where the individual is given a chance to shine.

Those Arians who do not enjoy playing sport may find walking or swimming good exercise, and many Arians will be found in the swimming baths during their lunch hours (and then eating their lunch on the way back to work!).

If they decide to lose a few pounds, the diet they undertake must show quick results, otherwise they will give up, as sustained discipline is not in their nature. Likewise, food will have to be quickly prepared and in generous portions – probably accounting for their above-average consumption of junk foods.

2

taurus

Taurus, 21 April – 21 May
Taurus is the second sign of the zodiac, and an earth sign, ruled by Venus. The sign for Taurus represents the strong face and horns of the bull.

Taurus is an earth sign and Taurean people generally have an interest in gardening and their environment. Female Taureans are particularly happy in the home.

Characteristics

Taureans are strong-willed, possessive, sometimes stubborn people, and very much like their Bull symbol. They are reliable, homely sorts who are happy when comfortable and secure. Security figures high on their list of priorities, and they dislike change of any kind; anything new is regarded with suspicion, and will be rejected in favour of the traditional and tried and tested. This dislike of change can often lead to holidaying in the same area year after year. Taureans have very fixed ideas, which they will seldom alter, even when pushed.

They are always there to lend a hand when needed. They are kind and understanding, and very good listeners, but sometimes they take this willingness to help and listen too far, and will become possessive and interfering, dominating if allowed.

They are fiercely protective of their families, and when their children leave the nest, Taurean mothers in particular will be constantly in touch, either on the telephone or visiting in person; they never get used to their offspring leaving home.

Fashion

Green, the colour of their birthstone, emerald, will often figure in their choice of clothes, as will tartans, tweeds and traditional fabrics.

Money Matters

Taureans are very methodical and practical; this includes a practicality with money. Hand in hand with their need for security, they will often plan for their old age, with an eye for investment in art, jewellery or antiques. Taureans like to feel safe. They value their home and will often go out of their way to create comfort. They are very patient and will wait until things can be afforded and not buy cheap things which won't last.

Improvements Needed

Taureans are renowned for their temper; like the Bull, they charge at those who have aroused their fury. They can often seem obstinate and stubborn, and are very slow to forgive an injustice. They have a good sense of humour, but are not very good at telling jokes. In their old age, Taureans have a habit of repeating things over and over again, and this includes jokes and things only they find amusing.

In The Home

Taureans love tradition in all its forms, from fashion through to politics. They are usually good cooks, but stick to traditional, favourite foods and recipes, preferring not to experiment. Often very good with their hands, female Taureans can be talented dress-makers and capable of making their own clothes. However, they take a long time to finish things, and often styles and sizes will have changed before the garment is ready to wear.

Their chosen birthstone is emerald, and things green, including plants and gardens, are very important parts of the Taurean's life. Many Taureans will have a perfect garden, and if not actually working in landscaping, could easily do so. They like things to be perfect, both inside and outside the home, and don't mind putting in the hours to achieve these aims. They are often great cooks and are very houseproud.

Partnerships

Taurus is a very sensual sign, but sometimes this passion can take a while to be aroused. Taureans will seldom be swept off their feet by a sudden romance, preferring to take things slowly. They are one of the least likely signs to have an affair, as they dislike anything which could disturb their security and stability.

In partnerships, Taureans are very faithful, with a yearning for old-fashioned romance. They are also very jealous people, and may try to suggest partners stay at home with them every night; freedom is not something they need or care about, and they assume that others feel the same. They may dislike parties, worrying that there may be people there who could find their partner attractive. They are not happy with living together relationships, as they don't fit in with their respect for tradition.

Marriage is important to Taureans – it isn't something to give up on, and they will stay with it, no matter what the problems. The only signs that they may not stick with are Geminians and Sagittarians, but they are unlikely to find themselves attracted to these star signs in the first place.

In terms of a permanent relationship or marriage, Taureans generally are best suited to the earth signs of Virgo and Capricorn. However, male Bulls are best matched from a romantic viewpoint with Libra and Scorpio whilst female Bulls are best matched for romance with Cancer and Libra.

Taureans as Parents

Taureans are naturally family people, concerned over their young-sters' welfare from the earliest moment all the way through to adulthood. To them, being a parent is a lifetime's commitment, and does not stop when the child grows up and leaves home. They will follow traditional parenting methods, wanting traditional schools, traditional interests and traditional standards for their children. Rules are important, and house rules will be set and must be followed to the letter.

Taureans are naturally affectionate, and their children will never go short of love or affection, and will always feel secure.

The Taurean mother is happy at home, and will bake and cook

for her children, often giving them large helpings of food which they are encouraged to finish before being allowed to leave the table. The Taurean's natural creativity and practicality will be encouraged in their offspring, and the child of a Taurean parent will often learn a great deal at home as well as at school.

Taurean parents will encourage their children to have a love and respect for nature, and will often take time to go out with their children in the countryside, pointing out items of interest and encouraging a love of the open air and walking in particular.

Education is important for Taureans, and they will buy as many books and works of reference as they can afford to help their child receive what they consider to be a proper, traditional education.

Whatever problems the children of a Taurean encounter, they can be sure that their Taurean parent will stand by them, listen patiently and then try to help as much as possible.

Generally speaking, Taureans get on well with all children, but they can have problems with Sagittarians, whom they find difficult to understand. One thing children of Taureans should remember is that Taureans feel children should be 'seen and not heard'.

Taureans as Siblings

Taurean children seem very adult and mature from an early age. They have a serious outlook on life and are conscientious in everything they do. They are generally tidy people, and, even as children, they will put their toys away rather than leave them around the house where they might get broken. They value their possessions from an early age and often have a reluctance to share their toys with others for fear of them getting spoiled or dirty.

With their natural love of gentle art-forms, many Taurean children will show an early interest in ballet and some grow up to enjoy yoga.

Taurean children are good, steady learners. They often display an interest in music and artistic pursuits because they can take their time with them and do them properly. They will work hard at school to achieve their aims; should they find themselves not living up to their own or their parents' ideals, they may suffer depression as a result.

As they grow up, Taurean siblings will become true friends and will always be there for you, but beware of takeovers – you could well go on holiday and come back to find your house re-organised – 'It needed tidying and I hadn't anything else to do so I just got started.' They mean well!

Taureans as Friends

If you have a Taurean friend, you have a friend for life, someone who will do all they can for you, you only have to ask. If you have a problem, they will get out their favourite tea pot and sit and listen.

If you are a Virgoan, your Taurean friend will be great fun and you will enjoy many happy hours together in creative pursuits.

Your Taurean friend, for the most part, will be easy going and affectionate. They will never flirt with your partner and you can be sure that should any advances be made to them, they will be repelled.

In a living together situation, Taureans will get on with most people, except Geminians and Sagittarians, and you can be sure that they will keep their part of the house tidy, even if you don't – but be careful they don't start tidying your things away too!

In a purely friendship relationship, they will get on well with Cancerians and Pisceans but Sagittarians' unrealiability will not lead to a happy partnership, nor will Leo's tendency to be boss all the time; otherwise Taureans will get on with most signs.

Taureans at Work

Those people who work for a Taurean boss will always feel comfortable in their office. Taureans tend to personalise their surroundings with touches of home – after all they feel happier at home than anywhere else. Often, the first thing they will do on arriving at work is to get a cup of tea or coffee, and many will have their own coffee percolator and a comforting supply of biscuits.

Taureans like order, and normally their desks will be tidy, at least by the end of the day if not all day. They will work hard to clear any backlogs before holidays and will leave full instructions for what is to be done in their absence.

They are good with money, are reliable and trustworthy, and are able to keep confidences.

If you have a Taurean as a boss, you can be sure that they will expect much of you, and if you break any rules, they will be very unforgiving. If you are late, you will be reprimanded in no uncertain terms, and if you turn up to work looking scruffy, you will be told. However, away from work, Taureans are friendly and open.

In most cases, Taurean bosses will follow the traditional methods of doing things. Many who are introduced to new computer equipment or things they consider 'new fangled' will go out of their way to discourage their purchase or use.

Taureans like everything and everybody to be as well organised and methodical as they are. Generally hard working, once given a task, they keep going until it is finished to their satisfaction, not settling for anything second best. Sometimes this leads to them taking longer to get things done than their colleagues – Aries people will always leave them standing!

They have no problem with being given a heavy work-load and, unlike others, will hardly ever make a fuss, even if they are asked to do a job which really belongs to someone else. They are very unlikely to be militant or interested in office politics. However, they are likely to find it difficult to block out trouble at home and problems at work can often be a sign of something wrong in their personal life.

Being practical people, they do well in practical jobs, and their love of the outdoors often leads to their taking jobs in building, gardening and architecture; their love of food can lead them to work in the food industry. Creativity plays an important part in their choice of job, and many Taureans work in the fields of music and art. Their ability to handle money could lead to jobs in banking, commerce or accountancy. Once a job has been chosen, they are likely to stay in the same job until retirement.

Taureans and Health

Many Taureans have weight problems. This is due mainly to their love of food in abundant quantities. However, weight problems will often not strike until later in life, when activity levels are reduced but food consumption is not. Then, with their natural determination, once they have embarked on a diet, they will stick to it, weighing portions religiously and counting calories. They should try to follow a low-fat diet which is high in fibre, and learn to watch portion sizes.

Taureans are seldom found in gyms working out. They like a little walking for exercise, rather than anything more strenuous. They love the outdoors, and rather than taking up aerobics or sport, they will work off excess weight by doing more around the house and garden, and then taking the dog for an extra long walk.

Dancing is a popular form of exercise for Taureans, and they may find they enjoy this for its own sake and for the element of socialising it provides. Many female Taureans will be involved in dance from an early age, and be good at dancing of all sorts.

Any changes in routine can cause stress and again this is something to be watched. Taureans often suffer badly with throat problems, tonsilitis, laryngitis, swollen glands in the neck, thyroid complaints and neck problems in general. Unkind people will often say that the female of the sign hardly ever stops talking, and this accounts for the throat problems they have, but that is unfair! Male Taureans may have a passion for rugby or wrestling, and will often find their neck areas subject to injury.

3

gemini

 ♊

Gemini, 22 May – 21 June
*Gemini – The third sign of the zodiac, and an air sign,
ruled by Mercury. The sign for Gemini represents the
numeral 2 in Roman lettering.*

Twins are communicative and self-expressive, qualities given by the
planet Mercury. They are active, adaptable and versatile, and very
inquisitive and humorous.

Characteristics

Gemini people are articulate but alarmingly inconsistent. They always
seem to be busy and need change and variety to be happy. Always

up-to-date and youthful in appearance, their intellectual nature needs to be challenged constantly. They are highly original and individual.

Gemini people are great talkers, and will happily spend hours on the telephone; they seldom seem to be at a loss for words. They make lively and amusing company, and their spontaneity can be infectious.

Bored by routine, they tend to flit from idea to idea and have a thirst for knowledge. Being sociable people, they often like to have other people around them to discuss their ideas, and to seek approval, which is important to them.

They love to browse in shops, and are very keen on anything which will make life easier for them.

Fashion

Fond of yellow and white, or any shade of lemon, Geminians will be very keen on the latest styles, and like streamlined, fitted clothes. Not particularly flamboyant dressers, they will go for clothes that look good and last.

Money Matters

Because they need variety, Gemini people will often have more than one job, and therefore more than one source of money. They are, however, not very good at budgeting, and should put some money away for a rainy day to compensate for their over-spending.

Improvements Needed

Gemini people should try to learn to be less impatient and restless. They often make losses because they fail to stay the course or see a project through to completion. They should also take time to listen rather than talk! They are naturally sympathetic, but can babble on too much.

The Home

As Geminians are not interested in having a show-home, preferring somewhere comfortable to relax in, their homes tend to be untidy, and if invited for a meal by a Geminian, expect something which hasn't taken too much time to prepare!

The women of the sign like feminine touches around their homes, and may often redecorate rooms in a short space of time as they get tired of the same surroundings. If they could move house frequently, they probably would. They may also want to constantly change the layout of their garden, or alter its appearance by having flowers which follow the seasons.

Geminians make good hosts, but may seem disorganised. They often have a hectic social life, with many different and varied interests.

Partnerships

Geminian people are naturally friendly, and have a large circle of friends. They value friendships, but also independence, and are often found joining clubs or taking up sports where new friendships can be made. Flirtatious by nature, Geminian people consider flirting with the opposite sex a game. However, sometimes others take them too seriously, and when in a permanent relationship, the flirtatious Geminian can cause difficulties. Faithfulness and Gemini do not go together.

Naturally drawn to other air signs and also Leo and Aries, Geminians often have holiday romances, or are tempted by brief affairs with work colleagues. They seem to have no serious side to them, and often marriage is not taken seriously either, with a decision to get married often being made on the spur of the moment.

If thinking in terms of a permanent relationship or marriage, female Geminians should look towards Librans and Aquarians for a good match, Leos and Arians for deep emotions and Scorpios for passion. Most other signs are best avoided, especially Cancer and Pisces – the Fish is likely to be a romantic attachment which unfortunately does not have staying power.

Male Geminians should look towards Librans, Virgoans and Leos for a good match, and Arians for a relationship with sparkle. They should avoid Capricornians and Taureans, as they would be dull and uninteresting combinations. Cancerians would provide a romantic relationship whilst Aquarians would be a true passion. Sagittarians may seem interesting, but there would need to be a lot of give and take for the relationship to work.

Two Geminians together will definitely need working at; the main problem being that they will both be spontaneous, but probably about different things at different times, but there would definitely be a lot of laughter! One of the couple would also need to learn to listen more, otherwise they will always both be talking at the same time.

Geminians as Parents

Geminian people never seem to grow up, and as a result make excellent, fun-loving parents, always very much in tune with their children. They will not care too much if the house is full of toys which never seem to be put away, nor will they mind a constant round of family outings.

Geminians value knowledge; often it is said that they are a mine of useless information! Consequently, they are very happy to buy books for their children, and it may often be the case that the person doing all the reading is the parent, rather than the child! They value education and will probably take a great interest in the schooling of their children.

A naturally warm and tactile sign, Geminian parents are full of praise and hugs for their children.

Geminian fathers are very good with small children, loving to tell stories and provide entertainment, but not so good with babies.

Geminian mothers are often eager to have a career and personal space, and this, combined with their dislike of housework, may encourage them to return to work fairly early on. However, any problem at home or with the children will mean they quickly return to the nest, often feeling guilty about not having been there when needed. Geminian mothers often employ child-minders, or ask willing relatives to help with the children so that they can continue their independent lifestyle.

Geminian parents will get on well with children from all signs, although they may find Taurean children's stubborn tendencies a problem and Capricornians' analytical nature difficult. Piscean children will also cause problems for them.

Geminians as Siblings

Geminian children make their presence felt. They enjoy most games and toys and love to play practical jokes. However, don't expect the Geminian sibling to put the toys away! Even the baby Geminian needs watching carefully, as they are very likely to want to explore.

They are unlikely to get on well with Cancerian children, and siblings who belong to this star sign are likely to be constantly at war with their Geminian brother or sister.

The main problem for Geminians seems to be that they lack concentration, and will be easily bored playing the same games over and over again. They will want, and need, a lot of stimulation. They can also be very competitive in family situations.

Geminian teenagers are likely to be lively, witty and happy, yet lack direction. They will look to others, including their family, for advice on career choices, but will end up making few decisions. They need to find something which is both challenging and full of variety.

Geminians as Friends

If you have the same interests as a Gemini, you are likely to get on well; Gemini people need to have friends who understand their interests and share their ideals. They like people who will take spur of the moment outings, go to lots of different places, and friends who will share gossip.

Geminians are great at parties. They particularly sparkle when asked to dress up, which allows them to take on a different personality and indulge their natural duality.

They like going to concerts and the theatre, and a friend who shares interests is likely to find themselves very busy! Don't worry about who does the driving, because Geminians like driving too, and are quite happy to take the wheel, especially on short journeys.

In a living together relationship, Geminians will get on well with other air signs and Arians. A Taurean with a Geminian, however, is likely to prove problematic.

If you are living with a Geminian, make sure you watch their use of the telephone – splitting the bills half-and-half will mean the Geminian is getting away with paying far less than their fair share – maybe a pay-phone would be a good idea.

In a purely friendship relationship, Geminians will get on best with Leos, Librans and Aquarians. They will find problems with Taureans and Capricornians.

Geminians at Work

Capable and versatile, Gemini people may never rise to great heights in their careers because they have too many other things to do. Once they do decide to concentrate on their career, however, and rise up the corporate ladder, the Geminian boss is likely to be full of new ideas, some quite revolutionary. However, they are also likely to be very disorganised, and need a good PA or secretary to keep them functioning effectively. They will be quite happy for staff to go to them with problems, and will be full of advice on how to make life easier. Geminian bosses will be happy to share their workload and delegate.

Gemini people are very likely to have work-related affairs, and being naturally flirtatious, there may be problems if there is an unattached Germinian boss around!

Geminians are often interested in 'get rich quick' schemes but also need some recognition for their work. Money will not be the 'be all and end all' for them. Above all, they need variety and will move swiftly from any job that is mundane or repetitious, or which demands silence, which is impossible for the Geminians! Indulging in chat or gossip is the only way some Geminians manage to stay in a boring job. In this respect, they are likely to work well with Arians, who also need plenty of noise and visual stimulus in their working environment.

Ideal jobs for the Gemini sign include working in communications, journalism (as either reporters or publishers), the media or entertainment. Gemini people are natural extroverts and very good mimics, so make excellent comedians and impersonators. All these types of jobs guarantee plenty of variety and excitement.

They also do well in jobs which involve travel, as again there is a constantly changing scene and lots of different people to meet. Many Geminians do well in sales-related jobs, and those which link sales with travel are likely to prove the most successful. Other suitable jobs include teaching, especially drama or sport, which allows the freedom to play a little, and counselling, as Geminians are very caring, and make good listeners. Their interest in travel can also lead to jobs within the transport industry. Even if they themselves don't get to travel, dealing with people that do will hold their interest.

Geminians and Health

Gemini people often have problems with joints – shoulders, hands and arms being the main problem areas. Many Geminians will have problems with their necks, due to tensions in and around their shoulders. They are also susceptible to problems connected with the chest, and often experience bronchial complaints, pleurisy or asthmatic difficulties. They also tend to suffer from rheumatic complaints, especially as they get older.

Naturally highly-strung and full of energy, they often need to watch their nerves, and should learn relaxation or meditation. Anything which causes upset to their home or family is likely to be a major cause of tension or stress. They can become very moody when family matters upset their plans.

They frequently use their natural energy in sporting activities, and are often good at tennis, badminton or squash; running may turn into a passion.

If embarking upon a diet, it is best for Gemini people to opt for one with plenty of variety and eat frequent snacks throughout the day, rather than three large meals. Diets, however, are seldom necessary, as Geminians rarely have weight problems; their only problems with food relate to eating too quickly and at the wrong times, and nibbling at biscuits and sweet or fatty things, like cakes and crisps, when bored.

Any exercise regime must be quick and easy, and preferably

not too demanding. Cycling is something that would fit in with the Geminian scheme of things. They would enjoy working out in a new gym, but they would do well to avoid taking up membership, as the novelty may well wear off before the membership is up for renewal.

As Gemini people often suffer from chest and/or lung problems, they would be well advised to learn breathing techniques.

cancer

 69

Cancer, 22 June – 23 July
*Cancer – The fourth sign of the zodiac, and a water sign,
ruled by the Moon. The sign for Cancer represents a crab's
claws.*

Crabs are by their very nature home-lovers, clinging, and sensitive
inside, like the crab itself. The Moon gives instinctive behaviour
patterns, intuition and a deep sensitivity.

Characteristics

Cancerians are very emotional, often putting up with difficult
situations and saying very little, repressing any urge to cause

4

28

trouble; they have a distinct dislike of confrontational situations. However, when on the defensive, they can be quite sharp with their tongues, in the same way as the crab will nip with its claws.

Cancerians are essentially loving, family people, very easily hurt and sensitive, but outwardly appearing totally in control. Security is important to the crab, and they will work hard to achieve their aims, avoiding taking risks and preferring to tread the traditional path. Good in business with good business sense, they make formidable opponents in both professional and personal matters.

They are blessed with a good memory for dates, events, historical details and trivia, but often have a problem being objective about their immediate, personal, situation.

Sentimental and reserved, they can often appear moody, but in a crisis, especially a family crisis, they will be sympathetic and helpful, and always there to lend a hand, even if it means forgoing their own plans.

Often artistic, Cancerians love their home, and will be quite happy to spend their time there while other members of the zodiac want to be going out. They are very patriotic and loyal.

Fashion

Lady crabs will generally be very smart, preferring subtle shades to bold and attention-grabbing colours. Clothes must represent value for money and tend to be conservative. Well-cut and well-tailored suits are likely to be popular, as are blouses and skirts, but flowing, soft, feminine styles are also likely to appeal, especially if green or blue, or representative of the sea.

Money Matters

Naturally careful with money, Cancerians count the pennies, will always know exactly how much they have, and will panic and become very uneasy should their bank balance fall below what to them is an acceptable level. They will most probably have a regular savings' plan or some money put away 'for a rainy day', and will always remember how much things cost, even years later! From an early age, they will start to make plans for their retirement, and will think of pension plans from the first possible moment. If you borrow money from a Crab, be sure to repay it to the penny!

Improvements Needed

The Cancerians' inability to see things objectively and be over-sensitive on occasions can cause problems, and they should try to work on this aspect of themselves. They also find it difficult to let go of situations, possessions and people who belong in the past.

In The Home

Family life is vital to the Crab, and they want their homes to be as secure and comfortable as possible. They like happy, warm atmospheres around them and will often spend a lot of money on their houses. Good in the garden in most cases, and also reasonably good cooks, they can be very private people, and possibly won't be 'neighbourly', regarding their homes as a personal territory.

They are notorious collectors and hoarders, and often their homes are full of things which have sentimental memories but little use.

They have a good sense of colour and their artistic leanings help to create a balanced home interior. Keen on music, they must have good quality sound equipment with a good quality radio.

Partnerships

Cancerians can be difficult to get to know, and often seem to have few real friendships. However, they are very caring once you take the time and effort to get to know them, and are extremely loyal and faithful and a tower of strength in times of difficulty. They sometimes seem to know what your problems are even before you tell them and they will try their utmost to help in any situation.

Not flirtatious or likely to be interested in having affairs, once they have committed themselves in a relationship, they are likely to stay. They can be very romantic and sentimental, and Cancerian men are extremely attentive to their partners.

They have a cool exterior, but beneath the mask is a very emotional person with strong feelings. Once in a relationship they can be very protective.

They are compatible with other water signs, apart from Pisceans who could cause problems, and get on especially well with fellow Crabs; they are unlikely to get on well with fire signs.

If thinking in terms of a permanent relationship or marriage, male Crabs should look towards other Crabs, avoid Taureans and Geminians and think twice about any fire sign. Librans might offer partnerships worth thinking about.

Female Crabs are likely to find Scorpios and Capricornians interesting (Capricorn being their opposite sign, and in this case opposites attracting), and again should avoid fire signs, with the exception of Arians, who are likely to provide very romantic relationships.

Cancerians as Parents

The Cancerians' naturally protective nature with regard to families and children can lead towards extreme possessiveness. They will endeavour to protect their children from any danger, actual or imagined, and can be very ruthless when other people cause problems for their children. They never forgive an injustice or slight, especially if it relates to their family.

They will feel very rejected if their offspring seem to distance them from their activities, or forget to telephone regularly – they care about other people, especially their children, and will want to spend time with them. This is especially true of Cancerian mothers. Cancerian parents will remind their offspring of the last meeting/telephone call/visit down to the hour!

Cancerian fathers may be difficult to understand. Sometimes distant and sometimes needing closeness, children of a Cancerian father often find it difficult to understand the need of their parent for his own space and his sudden moodiness. Naturally emotional, the Cancerian father is likely to be happy when his child is happy, sad when the child is sad, and it is not unusual for the male Crab to cry in front of his family when things go wrong.

Cancerians are, by nature, very proud of their families, and family history and tradition will be instilled in the offspring from an early age.

Cancerian mothers are naturally good mothers – warm, loving and caring. They are devoted to their offspring, and will happily do all in their power to create a loving and happy home environment and will spend time reading stories, playing and making tasty treats for their children. However, they can be very possessive, like Cancerian fathers, and may try emotional blackmail on their children to make sure they stay within the home environment. They don't like to feel left out and have a fear that something will befall their children if they are not there to prevent such a crisis, and in this respect, they are very like Taurean mothers.

Cancerians as Siblings

Cancerian children are very home-loving. They usually do well at school because they have good memories and kind natures, yet often need a lot of encouragement, thinking themselves less capable than they really are. They respect authority; this includes their parents and they are unlikely to be problem children.

If you grew up with a Cancerian brother or sister, you will know that they like to look after other people. These siblings will always seem to be older than you, even if they are not, and take time to make sure their fellow siblings are well cared for. This can cause problems, and may result in arguments, especially if one sibling feels undermined by their Cancerian brother or sister. Problems can also develop if the Cancerian's siblings want to play on their own. This will mean the little Crab feels rejected, and sulks and moods (and maybe tantrums) will result. Make sure that you don't move far away from your Cancerian sibling when you have a home of your own – they need to feel the family is close, even if this may not be the case.

Cancerians as Friends

They are sensitive and easily hurt by any sign of rejection – friends who forget their anniversaries or birthdays are likely to be unpopular; they never forget such things.

Naturally drawn to other water signs and the earth signs of the zodiac, they like people who enjoy peaceful pursuits rather than energetic go-getters, preferring to go for a walk with a friend rather than going to a disco. They are likely to find fire signs hard work.

Cancerians at Work

Very ambitious from an early age, the Cancerian will almost always know what he or she wants and go all out to get it. Once they have made it to the top, the Cancerian will be shrewd and tenacious, and probably make very sure that they have a good pension plan for the future. They may appear to be shy and introverted, but give them an objective, and they will not let you down. They are capable of working hard, and can be very hard on other people who do not come up to their expectations. Cancerians need to feel fulfilled in their jobs, that they are respected and liked; if they think they are being taken for granted, they will lapse into a sulk.

The Cancerian boss will be very protective of his employees and will make sure all his staff are happy and fairly paid. Responsibilities sit well with Cancerians and they ensure that the work environment is productive. They are tough bosses but sympathetic to their staff's troubles, and if an employee has problems at home, they are likely to try to help as much as they can. They are very sensitive to other people's moods; this may be partly why they need to try to help – they dislike 'atmospheres'.

In a situation where a Cancerian boss feels his workforce is not pulling its weight, or in the event of having to sack an employee, he may try to delegate his responsibility. Cancerians hate scenes and dislike confrontation; anything which they feel could lead to friction will be left, unless there is someone else to do it for them!

Being very private people, they are unlikely to want to indulge in office gossip and will guard any secrets well. Fellow-workers are unlikely to know anything that is going on behind the scenes; it is not that the Cancerian is devious, he is being protective.

Good careers for Cancerians include anything to do with the sea, catering, child-care, social work, nursing, commerce, banking, estate-agency, writing, hotel management or politics. If there is a family business, Cancerians will feel drawn towards that, even if it does not fit in with their personal inclinations or aptitudes.

Cancerians and Health

Cancerians are prone to worry, and this in turn leads to health problems. They may say little, but will think about things long and hard and work out every eventuality. Most of the things they worry about never happen, but they are always prepared for the worst.

They hate upsets and anything which unbalances the equilibrium will cause stress and tension to the Cancerian. Anything which upsets the home environment will also cause stress, and Cancerian parents are likely to fall foul of all sorts of minor illnesses when their offspring leave home.

There is a natural tendency towards stomach and digestive problems, with female Crabs often having problems with the breasts or womb, and problem pregnancies are not uncommon.

All Cancerians will fall prey to heartburn and indigestion, and really should watch their food intake and weight. Most Cancerians will have a weight problem, as they love good food and especially rich, fatty things. Any diet should be calorie controlled, as this will be easier for the Crab to cope with and will help them learn to control portion sizes. Cancerians get great pleasure from food, both preparing it and eating it, and love cream. They are often emotional eaters, and this is something they may have to battle against all their lives.

Any exercise programme will have to fit into the schedule, and probably walking to and from work would be enough to solve their weight problems. Cancerians are not very competitive, and sporting activities will be undertaken for enjoyment rather than any need to win. Their natural affinity with water may mean there is an interest in water-sports, swimming or even fishing.

5

leo

 ♌

Leo, 24 July – 23 August
Leo is the fifth sign of the zodiac, and a fire sign, ruled by The Sun. The sign for Leo represents the mane of the lion.

Leos are warm and sympathetic, yet demanding, assertive and intense.

Characteristics

Leo people are always on the go. They are the extroverts of the zodiac, and make their presence felt in all situations. They are not the wallflowers standing in the corner; they want to be noticed, and will be hurt if they feel rejected in any way.

Leos often seem overconfident, but in reality this is a mask hiding their sensitivity. They need constant reassurance and praise to be happy in their lives.

Like the Lion, their symbol, they are a regal sign, hating anything inferior and often spending a lot of money to create the right image.

They are romantics at heart, and will spend lavishly on their loved ones, male Lions often buying flowers or gifts for their mate. They can be very charming.

They are traditional in approach, exceptionally ambitious and idealistic, but also very sociable and good company.

Fashion

Likely to go for bright colours, reds, yellows and oranges (representative perhaps of the fire element), they like good clothes, will never buy anything they consider badly made or cheap and always look at quality. They are likely to go for designer labels if they can afford them, or at the very least something smart and well tailored. They are very particular about their clothes; everything must be well pressed and they must look well turned out at all times.

Money Matters

Money is important to the Leo but spending it is all so very easy; they have a great tendency to overspend, especially when things are going well for them. Extravagance, coupled with generosity, is second nature to the Leo. They are not the world's best at saving money or putting money aside for bills; and they tend to run short of money well before pay-day. This often leads to depression, as a Leo without money is not a happy soul!

Improvements Needed

Control of temper and of emotions is something which the Lion would do well to learn. Learning to control spending is another area for potential improvement. However, Leos' main aim should be to learn to take things in their stride and at the same time be a little less conventional, looking more towards different approaches to traditional issues. They should also learn to watch their demanding attitude where other people are concerned.

In The Home

The home of a Leo must be a place to relax and feel happy in, but it must also look right. They have very precise views on decor, and everything must be individual and stylish. Owning their own home is very important to the Leo.

When setting up a home for the first time, considerable thought will go into the furniture, which must match and be colour-co-ordinated. Leos have a great sense of style, and are often prepared to do-it-themselves to make sure that everything meets their required standard.

The garden is likely to be well looked after and well laid out, but not necessarily by the Lion. Supervising other people comes second nature to the Leo, and if they can afford to do so, many Leos will have a gardener, or just rely on an obliging spouse or relative! They like to have colour in their garden all year round, if possible.

Most Leos will have a pet, which is likely to have a great deal of affection lavished upon it and be thoroughly spoilt.

Partnerships

Leos are probably the most romantic people in the world. They fall in love deeply, and nothing is then too much trouble for their loved ones. Unfortunately, they tend to put the object of their affection on a pedestal, and this can be hard for the recipient to live up to. Should the loved one happen to slip from that pedestal, the Leo will seem totally lost and miserable, unable to cope with the situation.

A Leo partner must look good, behave well in company and be an excellent host or hostess. Above all, the partner must never take the limelight away from the Leo mate.

Basically faithful and loyal, they can become overwhelming, demanding and plain bossy in romantic situations. If they are rejected or spurned, they will be disconsolate and it will take a long time before their broken heart mends. They are exceptionally sensitive, and find it difficult to believe they could ever be at fault themselves.

Leos will generally find earth signs hard work, Taureans especially, seeming far too stubborn and unbending, and Scorpios and Cancerians can also cause problems. Both males and females are best suited to other fire signs, Gemini and Libra, but Leos may also be attracted to Aquarians. A female Leo with a male Virgoan is likely to be disastrous, and two Leos together may have a problem sharing the spotlight.

Leo people are not very good at keeping secrets in affairs of the heart and their very appearance gives them away every time. They are unlikely to have an affair simply for the prestige and a 'fling' is not very likely. They are all or nothing people.

Leos as Parents

Loving, warm and affectionate, Leos of both sexes very rarely have problems relating to children, unless the children happen to be Virgoans or Capricornians, in which case there are likely to be many misunderstandings.

As in any personal relationship, the Leo parent may spoil their child, but will be a hard taskmaster when it comes to house rules and regulations, and the child will have its own play area which is not allowed to encroach upon the remainder of the house or garden. Homework must be done, and bedtime will be strictly adhered to.

The Leo father in particular tends to spoil his children, and the family often comes across to outsiders as perfect and well-balanced, even if this is in fact not the case.

Leo mothers are exceptionally protective of their families, and will stop short at nothing to make sure the children are well cared for and well fed. They also realise the need for play and devote much time to playing with their children. Although many Leo mothers return to work after having their family, they will always be there when needed.

Leo parents will encourage their children to be independent and find answers for themselves and will be very proud of their offsprings' achievements.

Leos as Siblings

Leo children are larger than life, and always 'into something'. They have a compulsion to organise their siblings, and constantly seek praise and appreciation. Because of the Leo's need to shine at all times, their siblings often feel overwhelmed and rejected, and it is often better for the Leo child to be an only one! They tend to dominate their siblings, and those with a Leo brother or sister have to learn at an early age to stand up for themselves.

leo

Very loving towards a sibling who seems to need support or is quiet or withdrawn, Leo children will happily take physical action against anyone outside the family who upsets their brothers or sisters, and can become quite a bully. They can either be the little tyrant, or the happy child – depending on the amount of attention they are receiving.

Leo children love to play and may take an early interest in drama and performing, combining play with their need to be noticed. Leos of all ages have a good sense of humour, and dressing up comes naturally to them. They are natural performers, but need encouragement; if this is given by the parent to the young Lion, and not to his or her sibling, resentments can occur in the family.

As the Leo child grows up and learns to work with people rather than against them, their relationship with their siblings will probably be close. An interest in sports is likely to develop as the Leo child approaches maturity, and any sibling who shares this interest is made most welcome, provided that, in a competitive situation, the Leo is allowed to win.

In adult life, the Leo is likely to need a lot of reassurance in career matters and advice on relationships, and if the sibling is close, will ask for advice. Similarly, the Leo will be very supportive of the sibling should the need arise. It is a two-way process, which the Leo recognises.

Leos as Friends

Leos like having a good time. If you are friends with a Leo, you will most certainly have great times out on the town and have a lot of fun. Leos know how to let their hair down, and can be very witty and good company.

Leos don't seem to make friends easily. However the friends they make are likely to be friends for life. Possibly because they don't like people to see their sensitivities, Leo people often seem

41

to have a large circle of acquaintances rather than real friends; they like an audience, and this suits them well.

As friends they are reliable, kind and very supportive. They will give advice freely, which they expect to be followed to the letter. Nothing is too much trouble for the Leo friend – need a lift to the airport? Ask your Leo friend. Need a loan? Don't bother asking the Leo. They will already be overspent!

Leos at Work

Natural leaders, Leos will have a lot of ambition from an early age, but will not know which career to go into. All they know is that they must be successful and must have recognition for what they do.

Teaching is something which comes naturally to Leos, as does management. Working with young people or in sport will also appeal to them, as Leos never seem to get old in their ways and always have a good sense of fun. The entertainment industry is also likely to attract them, as they are natural entertainers. Many male Leos are drawn to military careers, again because they can be leaders. Female Lions may well have an interest in the fashion industry.

Leo people have a lot of confidence in themselves, and this can often help them into top jobs. They take pride in their work, work hard, put in long hours, have copious energy, and are very good at organising. They often feel success is theirs by right and as a result can seem arrogant and aloof when reaching high positions.

As a boss, the Leo is likely to have style. They are happy to join in and help those a rung or two down the ladder, but expect to receive respect and loyalty from their staff – woe betide anyone who fails to acknowledge this! They don't take too kindly to challenges from their staff, which they consider to be signs of disloyalty. They will not be told what to do by anyone; advice is one thing, but something which comes across as an order is quite another.

Making changes does not come easily for the Lion, and sometimes they need a push. If things go badly the Leo is likely to slip into a depression and will need a lot of support and encouragement. However, it is important to remember that the Lion likes to be the boss, even if this isn't always the case.

Leos and Health

Leos often have problems with their backs and their hearts. Despite their need for, and love of, success, when it comes, it can cause a lot of stress, and the Lion will start to suffer from backache and should watch for aches and pains in general. They will need to learn to slow down and be less demanding of their body. The need for frequent holidays and regular relaxation should be noted. Should there be emotional problems within the family, or a relationship difficulty, again the first sign will be the bad back.

Losing a member of the family causes a great deal of stress to the Leo; depression is likely to set in when someone close dies or in the event of a separation.

Diets may not be necessary for the Leo, as generally they have a high metabolic rate and are normally pretty fit. However, should they need to lose weight, they must make sure they allow for a little indulgence each day, whether this be food-related or a treat of some other kind. Food matters to the Leo, and going out for meals is something which takes on a great deal of importance, when finances permit. This can be the one cause of overweight for the Leo. Generally speaking, they like plain food, but are often tempted by sweet things and fruit (especially dried fruit).

Exercise is fairly important for the Lion. Working out or 'training' is likely to be well organised and well structured. Anything competitive will appeal, provided they are the leaders of the group and their team wins in the end.

6

virgo

Virgo, 24 August – 23 September
Virgo – The sixth sign of the zodiac, and an earth sign, ruled by Mercury. Virgo, the virgin is the only sign relating to the female human form.

Virgoans are passive people, well controlled and practical, and liking order. They are sharp-witted and have a dry sense of humour. They can be introverted.

Characteristics

Virgoans are very discriminating people, critical yet fair. They can be very fussy and overprecise, demanding attention to detail and worrying unnecessarily about trivialities. They are, however, very efficient, practical people, and put in charge of a project or a group of people, they perform quickly and well.

Virgoans are generally shrewd and often succeed in business. To outsiders, and people who don't know them well, they can seem cold and aloof, yet they are very caring, helpful people.

Never saying things they don't mean, and never meaning things they don't say, Virgoans don't like being centre-stage. They prefer to be working in the background, leaving the limelight free for people like Leos. Sometimes, Virgoans can be downright introverted.

If they are asked to research a subject, they will not stop until they have covered all aspects. They are very adaptable, and happily accept a large workload, knowing that they have the intellectual capabilities to deal with a wide range of mental disciplines.

They are blessed with retentive memories, never forget birthdays, names or important information, are not likely to gossip and can be trusted with secrets.

Virgoans often prefer to work to schedules. They tend to pigeon-hole their lives and like order and routine.

Fashion

Virgoans are cautious, conventional and practical in the way they dress. They are not likely to overspend on clothes, and look for economy and bargains. As with most things, Virgoans are restrained when it comes to buying clothes, and are likely to choose colours which mirror their earth sign (i.e. soft browns and greens) and lightweight fabrics.

Money Matters

Organisation is paramount to a Virgoan. Consequently, it should come as no surprise that they are very well organised financially. They dislike taking risks or cutting corners and are likely to have savings' accounts, pension schemes, life assurance and the like. Their money is invested wisely and well. They are not prone to extravagances of any kind; they are unlikely to ever need an overdraft.

Improvements Needed

The Virgoans' need to analyse everything can cause no end of problems, especially when they go on to worry about what they have found. They should learn to be more relaxed and open in their attitudes. There is nothing wrong with talking problems through with other people; more often than not, other people want to help just as much as the Virgo does. They should try to be less obsessive about everything being perfect, and should learn to be more confident and self-assertive.

In The Home

The decor in the Virgoan home will be subtle, and probably favour the colour white. It looks clean, and cleanliness matters to the fussy Virgoan. They are good with interior design, and their homes are comfortable and well furnished.

The Virgoan home is normally well organised, efficiently run and tidy, and Virgoans are likely to be the first to apologise for something seeming to them to be out of place. They have very high standards and dislike imperfection in anything.

Being artistic, many Virgoans are keen on pottery, and if not actually capable of making their own, they are likely to have a lot of pottery around their homes, as well as glass objects and other small items. They like to collect things which come in sets and female Virgoans may spend years collecting individual pieces of china to make a full dinner service.

Generally speaking, they like gardening, from weeding through to planting shrubs and bushes, and their gardens will be tidy and well looked after and most of all, planned, so that there are plants coming into bloom and giving colour throughout the year. Male Virgoans are very practical and likely to have a lot of gardening and DIY equipment, and may even go to evening classes to improve their skills.

Partnerships

Basically shy and inhibited, Virgoans are likely to find it difficult to show their emotions. They tend to spend a lot of time analysing the motives of the other party before deciding to commit themselves. Essentially self-conscious, Virgos are not romantics, fearing rejection.

Faithful and loving with the right partner, they have a tendency to nag and find fault if their partner does not come up to their expectations at all times.

Naturally drawn to Capricornians and Taureans, Virgoans are unlikely to have affairs. They may find Cancerians and Scorpios interesting, but Scorpios' high sex-drive may cause them problems. They are unlikely to get on very well with Sagittarians, and dreamy Aquarians are likely to have to bear the brunt of a lot of nagging, should a relationship develop.

Female Virgoans are likely to find themselves happier with Geminians than their male counterparts would; Virgoans and Arians are likely to make for potentially explosive relationships.

Virgoans as Parents

A Virgoan parent is well organised and expects the children to be the same – they must learn to organise their time and be well behaved, as the Virgoan parent was in its own childhood. They must also learn to be tidy and put away their toys when playtime is over. The Virgoan mother, in particular, is likely to have a lot of problems with an untidy child and may well end up with a nagging headache. However, if a child comes to the Virgoan mother with a real problem she will deal with it efficiently, effectively and calmly. However, should the child fall ill, even have a slight cold, the Virgoan will rush straight to the doctor, fearing something terminal even when outward signs suggest only a minor disorder.

Virgoans are likely to have small families. Probably aware of the mess that children can create, they see large families as illogical. Virgoans tend to remain young at heart, and so relate well to children in general, but should the Virgoan parent have a Leo, Aries or Sagittarius child, problems are inevitable.

The Virgoan father is likely to have strict rules and routines, which must be followed at all times.

Education will be important to the Virgoan parent, and the father in particular is likely to expect his child to do well at school, study when at home and pass every examination – the Virgo parent liked school, so the offspring should too!

Aware of the need for sufficient funds to pay for all the things they want and consider necessary for their family, Virgoan mothers are likely to continue to work, or take a part-time job to ensure financial security.

Virgoans as Siblings

Virgoan children are tidy children. They won't like a sibling who is untidy or dirty. They are very analytical, and are likely to take their toys apart to find out how they work. However, being very practical, they will probably be able to put them back together again, and may use the information gained to go on to adapt their toys or even make new ones.

They are very home-based children, and are quite happy to stay around the house rather than going out to play with their siblings. Sometimes, they have a tendency to become a 'Mummy's boy' or a 'Mummy's girl' and can seem cold and too perfect to their brothers and sisters. Should the Virgo child have a fire sign sibling, look out for fireworks – Virgoan children like routine and order and have little time for egos.

A Virgoan sibling is a blessing in a crisis; they will always be there with good, sound advice and help. Likely to be good at school, the Virgo child will work hard, but will have a difficult time when leaving school and deciding upon a career.

Virgoans as Friends

Virgoans are supportive and loyal and make good friends. They are likely to form close friendships with Cancerians and Scorpios, as well as with other earth signs: Virgos are, however, slow to make friends, as their sometimes caustic wit causes problems and they have a natural tendency to criticise.

You can also be sure that you will always hear the truth from them; Virgoans are very truthful and honest, and they will keep any secret you tell them.

Essentially wise and sensible, any advice offered by a Virgoan is likely to be well thought through. Sympathetic and caring, the Virgoan will provide a good shoulder to cry on, and will be an excellent nurse, should this be necessary. However, watch out for their natural tendency towards hypochondria.

Virgoans at Work

With their liking of detail, order and routine, highly organised and structured professions are likely to appeal to the Virgo as a career. Publishing, administration, computers, secretarial work, nursing, writing (a passion for Virgos), designing, statistics, theatre, accountancy – all these areas are well suited to the Virgoan temperament and interests.

They are unlikely to want to run their own business, yet are happy to work long and hard for their employers, often starting at the bottom and working their way up the ladder. They can become workaholics, liking everything done properly and efficiently and not wanting to delegate to anyone else for fear of their own high standards being compromised.

They are often happy to put forward proposals without receiving the credit; as long as they believe in what they are doing, they are likely to be happy in their work.

Demanding perfection of themselves and others, they will take on the mantle of boss only with reluctance. They often become obsessed with detail, and their staff will have to comply with this necessity to look at everything with a fine-tooth comb. They will also have to be punctual, tidy, and well organised. Often the extra responsibility that management brings can lead the Virgoan into nervous problems due to stress and tension. However, they are always happy to listen to anyone's problems and they will be a caring boss.

Virgoans and Health

Virgoans worry about their health. Health is a great concern; the slightest cold will be taken seriously and appropriate measures taken.

Likely to suffer from stomach problems (probably related to stress), they are also liable to ulcers, indigestion, heartburn and appendix-related problems. Their inability to relax and unwind at the end of a day at work often result in sleep problems. They should learn meditation or relaxation techniques to help, and try to stop being so self-critical.

Virgoans know all about nutrition. They read up on the subject and are careful about the food they buy and the food they and their families eat. They are normally good cooks. They dislike anything fried, and prefer savoury to sweet foods. Should a diet become necessary, which is only likely if they have been worrying a lot and have been eating for comfort, the Virgoan will happily list everything they eat (with the calorie or fat content by the side), probably even going as far as to weight everything meticulously. They diet well, as the organisation involved keeps their interest and appeals to their sense of order.

They are unlikely to want to take up any sport for exercise, but are keen to keep fit, and will probably visit the local gym or exercise at home. Male Virgoans may have an interest in golf, but probably will not be regular visitors to the clubhouse.

Anything which causes change in their lives is likely to be a problem for Virgoans and they are more prone to stress-related problems than almost any other sign.

7

libra

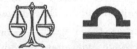

Libra, 24 September – 23 October
*Libra – The seventh sign of the zodiac, and an air sign,
ruled by Venus. The sign for Libra is representative of the
scales, equally balanced. It should be noted that the symbol
for Libra is the only inanimate object amongst the signs,
all other symbols being representative of man or beast.*

Librans seek for a balance in all situations. They need to weigh up
all situations before coming to a decision and seek harmony at all
costs.

Characteristics

Librans are diplomatic people, disliking upset and discord, and doing their utmost to avoid conflict situations. They are fair and just but can be unforgiving; resentments last a long time.

They like people. Being compassionate and understanding, they like to look after others and be helpful but they have a dislike of large crowds. They often crave the company of other people and always prefer small group activities to doing anything alone.

Needing approval, they will take care over their appearance. They like the niceties of life, whether this be clothes, food or surroundings, and never think of shopping for anything cheap. They demand quality, and are perfectionists in all things. A small rattle in the car will have to be thoroughly investigated and put right immediately – after all, it means that the car is not perfect!

They have very strong opinions and once a view has been formed they will not shift from their standpoint. However, they can also be very indecisive, and take a long time to come to a decision. If you ask a Libran what they would like to drink at a party, you must be prepared for quite a wait while they decide.

Librans, however, do occasionally like to do things on the spur of the moment, and will gladly take a last minute holiday, or go off on a whim without thinking about whether they can afford it or not first.

Fashion

Librans are very conscious of fashion and colour. By nature refined, Librans are unlikely to go for anything outlandish and prefer clothes to be fashionable yet not too bold. Pretty clothes in subtle shades are likely to appeal to the female Libran. They don't follow fashion to the last detail, preferring to make their minds up about what suits them and what doesn't.

Librans may not have huge wardrobes, but what they have will look good and will last. Both sexes are likely to be immaculately turned out at all times.

Money Matters

Librans enjoy shopping. They enjoy buying nice things and having nice things around them. To this end they will happily spend money on themselves and Librans may find they overspend quite easily, have regular overdrafts and often be up to their limit on their credit cards.

Less well-off Librans may be jealous of anyone around them who is doing better than they are. They want to have all the nice things they see that others have, and can be very envious of their neighbours and friends, especially when it comes to cars. However, they are ambitious people, and will work hard to get the money they feel they deserve.

Improvements Needed

Librans should try to be more decisive. They have a great tendency to wait for others to make the first move and this can make them seem lazy, which is not really the case, and can make them seem to change direction alarmingly.

Librans can be very introverted and lacking in confidence. They may have ambition but do not always have the drive of some other members of the zodiac to pursue their aims to the end.

The tendency to be extravagant with money and buy things they can't afford should also be watched. They must learn that the fact that something costs a lot does not mean it is necessarily good value; Librans need to look past the price ticket. Female

Librans should realise that they don't really need to spend such a lot of money on beauty products.

In The Home

As soon as you step foot inside a Libran home, you feel you have entered somewhere special. It is important to Librans to make their homes look as good, comfortable and as balanced as possible, and even if they can't afford to have a large house, they will make the most of what is available, and try to furnish it in elegant, subtle and fashionable materials balanced with traditional styles.

However, don't expect the Libran to do all the hard work themselves. If they can afford to employ a decorator or interior designer they will most certainly do so, and will make sure that they work to strict guidelines on colour and style, although perhaps not on cost. It is vitally important to the Libran that everything matches and that colours do not clash. The Libran home is a place into which to escape from the drudgery of the world at large.

Librans dislike noise, and prefer a property tucked away in a backwater to something in the town or city-centre.

The Libran home is likely to have a lot of paintings in it. Librans enjoy art, and will buy anything beautiful which takes their fancy when on a shopping spree. It is important that things look good, and if one of the paintings is not straight, the Libran will notice and straighten it immediately.

Gardens are also important to the Libran. They must have a balance of colour rather than random splashes of colour here and there. Landscape design is one of their interests, and they may spend a long time planning their garden and visiting garden centres to see what is available.

Partnerships

Harmony, romance and love are essential to the Libran, and at the very heart of their existence. This, unfortunately, can often lead to infatuation, early and unhappy marriage, or, conversely, to a long period of bachelorhood while waiting for the right person to come along.

Natural flirts, even within a happy relationship, Librans are likely to get on well with most signs, with the exception of Cancer, Scorpio and Capricorn. More likely to have an affair than most other signs (except perhaps Scorpio) Librans need to feel loved and wanted, and fall in love easily. Probably the best match for any Libran would be with an Aquarian or Geminian, with Leo coming a close third. Two Librans together are likely to get nothing done, and this is not an ideal partnership.

Librans are good friends, and being a good partner is important to them. They have a good sense of humour but are often reluctant to use their own wit and prefer to be in the company of humorous people who will make them laugh. Librans like to entertain but not be in the spotlight.

Librans as Parents

Librans like to fuss over people, and that includes fussing over their children. As a result, although very loving, Libran parents are likely to be too accommodating and too easy-going. They will to do anything to keep the peace and often it is the children in the household who rule the roost, rather than the Libran parent. It is important for Librans that everything is well balanced and pleasant and they will try to instil these traditional values in their children, who must be polite, well mannered and quiet but sociable.

Libran parents expect their children to look good, and will

encourage their children to value beauty. Anything artistic is likely to be encouraged. Libran fathers are probably not overtidy and there will be a tendency for the children to take after him, irrespective of their own zodiac sign.

Libran mothers may come into parenthood late in life and regard motherhood and its responsibilities as a serious profession. Unlikely to ever shout at her children, despite temptation to do so, her children will nevertheless have to toe the line and do as they are told.

Librans get on well with most children, and are unlikely to have problems with their own offspring, as any argument is likely to be glossed over so that harmony returns as quickly as possible.

Librans as Siblings

Needing lots of encouragement from an early age, the Libran child is likely to be well behaved and co-operative. This may not go down too well with the siblings of the Libran, who may see their brother or sister as a goody-goody, never argumentative, always neat and tidy, always well-behaved and always seeming to be popular with adults. The Libran's need for balance is inbred and is obvious from the outset.

As the child develops, the family is likely to appreciate the Libran child, who will gladly help out with meal preparation, tidying up and helping generally. The child is unlikely to enjoy sport and any sign of interest needs the encouragement (and participation perhaps) of both parent and sibling to get off the ground. Team activities suit the Libran best. If the Libran child thinks too much about it, the chances are the whole project will be shelved. If they are bullied, however, they are likely to go along with a project just to keep the peace, despite not really wanting to take part, and will end up feeling resentful.

Librans as Friends

Librans are good friends, wanting to help as much as possible, and becoming distressed at any situation which seems to be causing problems for their friend.

Librans get on with most people, and would adapt to living with any other zodiac sign, as they have a tendency to build their lives round other people and do what they think is best for them.

Librans at Work

Librans need to work in a happy atmosphere. Anything strained, noisy, dirty, or untidy is likely to have little appeal and leave the sensitive Libran feeling miserable. A little noise is vital, but too much noise will create tension. An airy, well-ventilated and light working environment is essential for the Libran.

Librans only seem genuinely unhappy at work when others are in bad moods and will not compromise or if their energy levels drop (to counteract this, Librans tend to drink large amounts of coffee and tea throughout the day to maintain their caffeine levels).

Librans work well in planned situations and need to make sure everyone in the workplace is happy. They hate to think people don't like them, yet when one of their moods strike, it is little wonder work colleagues lose patience with them.

Anything worthy of debate will produce a happy response from Librans, who love mental stimulation and anything which challenges their patience. Not content to wait for success, Librans are likely to be attracted to 'get rich quick' schemes, especially if their partner suggests it is a good idea.

Being naturally diplomatic, Librans are excellent in any job requiring diplomacy, such as public relations, counselling, welfare or social work. Their love and appreciation of beauty would also make them good hairdressers or beauticians and anything in the art, design, or fashion worlds would also be of interest.

As a boss, the Libran is likely to be very conscious of the welfare of his or her staff, yet be surprisingly stubborn on occasions and well suited to the task of making others toe the line. The only problem in working for a Libran is when there are choices or decisions to be made. Likely to think about the outcome before making the decision, quick answers will not be forthcoming. Likewise, any firing of staff is liable to produce a 'dither', as the Libran will be aware of the effect on the employee concerned; they like everyone to be happy.

Librans and Health

Likely to suffer with low-back pain, sensitive or problem skins, nervous complaints and kidney or bladder problems, Librans do not react well in stressful situations, especially if they affect themselves personally or their families. If there is a problem at home, the Libran will be useless at work, and separation or divorce is likely to see them very unhappy and miserable. Likewise, making a choice between two relationships will make them exceptionally tense, as will having no relationship at all, at which time they tend to eat for comfort. Indeed, Librans who are depressed are immediately obvious as they tend to be constantly eating. Often settling for harmony at a cost to themselves, Librans get easily upset, leading to loss of good health and well-being.

Librans like their food, but it has to be well prepared, attractively served and have a delicate taste. However, give them chocolate or biscuits and they are easily satisfied, as they will also be with anything creamy. They certainly have a sweet tooth!

Female Librans in particular like to entertain, and if they do this too often, or go out for too many meals (another thing they love) a diet may be necessary. If embarking on a diet, the Libran will always join a club or group as they like both the company of fellow-dieters and the competitive element. They will eat a lot of salads and cut down on portion sizes, abandoning anything too creamy. However, they are unlikely to want to go to exercise classes and will want to go walking or take up something like tennis which can be played with other people and is not too rough.

8

scorpio

 ♏

Scorpio, 24 October – 22 November
*Scorpio – The eighth sign of the zodiac, and a water sign,
ruled by Pluto, but also associated with Mars. The sign for
Scorpio represents the legs and tail of the scorpion.*

Scorpios are intense people, secretive, intuitive and passionate, often
exuding a mystical quality and inner depth, Pluto's influence tends
to lead to rebirths at various stages of their lives and Mars influ-
ences the direction and intensity of their very nature.

Characteristics

It is said that a Scorpio can be spotted easily by looking at their eyes, which seem to have a mystical quality. Whether you agree with this or not, Scorpios certainly have a magnetism (often of a sexual nature), a seemingly boundless degree of energy, and a perception which is clearly defined.

Anything old, mystic or deep is likely to appeal to the Scorpio, yet strangely they are often sceptics when it comes to astrology.

Scorpions are intense people with deep emotions and once they take up a cause, they will stay with it to the bitter end, sometimes becoming quite obsessive.

If they feel wronged, the Scorpion will embark on a plan of revenge and can be very secretive and purposeful. They will analyse situations and work things through in great depth.

Fashion

Scorpions are not flashy in their dress – they often wear something which is dramatic but not too bold, as they dislike anything ostentatious. Despite this, however, the Scorpion is always noticeable. Often female Scorpions will choose something sexy and clinging, which accentuates their figure, and like dark colours. Male Scorpions are likely to wear casual clothes at every opportunity and especially like clothes which are sporty but smart.

Money Matters

Scorpions are unlikely to gamble or speculate to accumulate their money. More likely, they will work quietly and effectively and hope they will eventually make the kind of money they would like. Having acquired money, they will not buy flashy new clothes or cars, as they consider this vulgar and ostentatious.

Generous when things are going well for them, Scorpions enjoy the feeling of power and will be able to manipulate situations to the best advantage. They are very astute and perceptive, and rarely miss anything, often succeeding with business ventures where others have failed to recognise possibilities.

Not likely to spend a fortune shopping, unless something really appeals, Scorpions can be very thrifty and will plan carefully to have a comfortable retirement and old age.

Improvements Needed

Scorpios can be very blunt and argumentative when the mood takes them, and this is something which should be watched, together with their tendency towards dominance over others and their apparent need for power.

They should learn that it is acceptable to be more open about their emotions and that in times of trouble other people are there who can help.

Learning to cope with resentment is something which Scorpions would do well to address. They can be very vindictive and jealous, and are capable of being cruel at times, often bearing grudges far too long.

In The Home

Scorpions value their homes and like to create surroundings which are private, clean, warm and tastefully decorated and furnished. Often they will prefer an old house to a modern one – they like the chance to make a property individual, and restoration work is of great interest to them. They are not averse to doing the necessary work themselves in order to achieve the look that they are after. Many Scorpions have a restlessness which leads them to move house fairly often; once they have done up their home, they may start looking around for another house and do the same all over again.

Having a garden is not essential to the Scorpion. Many will settle quite happily for a window box and a few herbs growing in the kitchen. However, if the property they buy comes with a garden, they are likely to enjoy it and set about organic gardening, with a large compost heap, and probably a pond too. They will make sure it is very private and either erect a tall fence or plant quick-growing conifers to provide the seclusion they prefer.

Scorpios are unlikely to be neighbourly. They are very much loners, and prefer to sit at home and read rather than get involved in community affairs.

Partnerships

Love is a serious business to the passionate Scorpio. They often have a high sex-drive, and are very romantic with the right partner. However, they often take a long time before finally settling down into a permanent relationship. They spend years 'playing the field' and enjoy every minute of it.

Jealousy and possessiveness is something which goes hand in hand with having a Scorpio partner. Often finding it difficult themselves to be open about their emotions, they are suspicious of other people and take time to relax into a relationship. If a partner wrongs them in any way, they will be very ruthless and try to get their own back. They are volatile, and likely to be possessive, and insecure, needing a lot of reassurance and support.

Scorpios will most likely find other water signs and also earth signs interesting but are unlikely to become too attached to either Leos or Aquarians.

Affairs are more than a likelihood for Scorpions, who will rarely draw the line at a little sexual fun. However, once married, the Scorpio will seldom stray. Making a vow is a serious undertaking for the Scorpion, who would never wish to be seen to go back on a promise. They, in turn, would be horrified if their partner were unfaithful; they don't believe in sharing, on any level.

In a business partnership, beware of rivalry from the Scorpion. Cancerians, Pisceans and Aquarians may work well with the Scorpio subject, but most other signs are likely to find the competitive element too exacting and the deviousness too much to bear. The best partnerships for the Scorpion are likely to be with Pisces and Aries.

A relationship with a Gemini subject will most likely prove disastrous, as will two Scorpions together – there will be too many secrets and too much mistrust for the relationship to stand a chance of success.

Scorpios value their privacy and are unlikely to enjoy sharing a property with someone on a platonic basis.

Scorpios as Parents

A Scorpio parent will be strict; there will be rules to be followed and obeyed. They may appear to their offspring as quite detached emotionally, unless some reward is due, in which case the Scorpio will make quite a fuss. They are often very proud of their children and can equally be very possessive. The need to protect their young is fundamental and they realise in an instant if something is troubling their child. They provide good shoulders to lean on in times of trouble.

Scorpio parents need to know what their children are up to at all times. As a result, they can often seem to spy on their children.

Scorpios get on well with Libran children, but Cancerian, Aquarian and Virgoan children may prove difficult to understand; Geminian children may seem quite impossible to them.

Scorpios enjoy competition and are fairly active in a sports sense. A child who has an interest in sports will be encouraged.

Most Scorpio fathers are likely to have their own sanctuary

somewhere in the house – whether it is a study or a garden shed; it is necessary for them to have somewhere private, and the child of the Scorpio must realise this, and never, ever intrude.

Scorpion mothers aim to be the perfect mother. They are full of energy, enthusiasm and protective spirit. However, this can cause problems at times, especially if their child is sensitive or quiet, when they will become critical and over-protective.

Scorpios as Siblings

A Scorpio child will always prefer his or her own company and as a result may seem very detached from any siblings. However, don't assume that they don't care about their brothers and sisters because that would be far from the truth. They care deeply and are very sensitive but, on occasions, they can also be very cruel to their siblings. They are very quiet children who often need to be alone, and may feel threatened by the sibling who pushes too hard or seems to demand too much attention from the parent.

School is likely to be a mixed experience for the Scorpion. Sports events will be loved, especially anything aggressive, like martial arts. Anything scientific will also appeal.

Scorpios are very good at keeping secrets, and if the sibling has a need to confide in the Scorpion brother or sister, rest assured that the secret will never be divulged. However, the Scorpion will find it difficult, if not impossible, to share emotional problems with anyone, even the sibling, and so the traffic is likely to flow one way only. If there is a problem to be solved, give it to the Scorpio child, and you will keep them happy and make them feel more secure and needed.

As they grow up, Scorpio children often have difficult times, especially in adolescence, when they take a lot of time finding their feet. As a result, their siblings may feel perplexed by the Scorpio child, who is really just frustrated. Encouragement and discipline will work wonders and the Scorpio child will respond and relax. However, should the sibling seem to be doing well and the Scorpio child is having problems, resentment and jealousy will creep in and be very difficult to dismiss. In later life, it is often the case that the Scorpio will feel guilty for his or her behaviour and try hard to heal any rifts which have developed.

Scorpios as Friends

Scorpios are often reluctant to make the effort to get to know other people due to their natural suspicion over the motives involved. For this reason, most Scorpios are likely to have a number of acquaintances yet few close friends. Those people who are lucky enough to count a Scorpio amongst their friends are likely to value the friendship, as Scorpios are loyal and willing to help out whenever they can. Above all, they will keep any secrets you care to tell them and become long-standing, good companions.

Sometimes very difficult and seemingly uncompromising, Scorpions often relate best to water signs and earth signs. Fire signs, present a problem, as they are too extrovert; air signs are likely to be too logical.

Scorpios at Work

Naturally intuitive, especially in business, Scorpions often end up in charge of large concerns. Power and control are important to them, and they have huge amounts of energy and drive to help them get to the top in any career they choose. They seem to know when to push forward and when to hold back, when to expand and when to consolidate. They are expert at dealing with the un-expected or the unforeseen, and cope well and calmly in crisis situations. They can be very ruthless when necessary and often thrive on disruption. On the way up the ladder of success, the

Scorpio may employ devious tactics to make their mark. They will work hard and with commitment and anyone who fails to notice this will meet with contempt from the Scorpio. They will be very competitive and rivalries are almost inevitable.

When, not *if*, they become boss, the Scorpio is likely to be a difficult taskmaster. They will expect a lot from their employees, be very unbending, and at times seem to expect the impossible. However, they have great respect for those who work hard and are thorough. Although they rarely share their own plans with anyone, they will always know exactly what everyone else is doing.

Scorpios have a natural interest in health and herbalism and jobs in the medical profession will appeal. They are also very analytical and enjoy research, so policework, archaeology and psychology are also good career choices. Many Scorpions are drawn to mystic interests, and may find themselves working as tarot readers or palmists or may just be interested in psychic detection and investigation as a hobby.

Scorpios and Health

Scorpios are likely to have trouble with their bladder, kidneys and genital areas, as well as having nasal problems. Many female Scorpios will have menstrual difficulties and suffer badly from PMT, yet sail through pregnancy with little trouble, other than fluid-retention problems.

Stress is seldom likely to be felt, and then only when there is outside pressure to do something against their will or when their privacy is invaded.

Despite their love of food, which can lead to excessive eating, the Scorpio is unlikely to ever have to diet. This is because they can be very disciplined after over-eating. If it is necessary at any stage to diet, the Scorpio will tell nobody but just cut down on the creamy things they love and religiously count calories, rather than join a slimming club or take up extra exercise.

Most Scorpios are very fit. They like water sports and anything competitive will have a huge appeal – they don't do anything just for the fun of taking part. They are very disciplined when it comes to any form of exercise programme and can become quite obsessive.

sagittarius

Sagittarius, 23 November – 21 December
Sagittarius, the ninth sign of the zodiac, and a fire sign, ruled by Jupiter. The sign for Sagittarius is representative of the bow and arrow, with the archer depicted as half man and half horse.

Archers are energetic, assertive and extrovert, with an openness and restlessness and need for freedom and their own space. Jupiter gives them a desire for expansion and growth and they can be very ambitious.

Characteristics

Archers are always totally honest and sincere, and are generally optimistic about everything. However, at times they can be gullible and absent-minded, and their powers of concentration are sometimes found to be lacking.

Firey, outspoken and adaptable, they often make quick decisions which can however, sometimes prove to be wrong. Sagittarians work equally well either for an organisation or for themselves, and like the opportunity to look after other people.

Naturally intuitive and humourous, these people seem to follow an easier path in life than many of their contemporaries, yet often decide around the age of forty to do something completely different with their lives, much to the chagrin of their families, and often embark upon a journey of discovery which encompasses new customs, cultures and countries. They enjoy anything which involves adventure.

Fashion

Casual dress often appeals to the Archer, and whilst not particularly fashion-conscious, they will always be fairly well dressed especially on an evening out. Colourful things will attract them (reds especially) as will anything with a sense of the dramatic. Sporty clothes will have the most appeal and anything which looks like a bargain will be a must.

Money Matters

Sagittarians often take risks with money, and gambling can be a major part of their lifestyle. As a result, Sagittarians either seem to have a lot of money, or none at all. However, their natural optimism will not cause them to be concerned about their financial status, as there will always be something coming along which could improve matters. Any money lost as a result of speculation will not be mourned, as the adventure of the enterprise will have been the main motivation.

Improvements Needed

Being too honest, open and blunt can lead to problems for the Archer, who is often seen as tactless or boastful. Archers should learn to think first and speak afterwards, rather than the other way round, and to make sure of all their facts before speaking. They are very impulsive and rash, and this causes no end of difficulties in their lives. They should try to avoid being extreme and seeing everything as either black or white. They also need to learn to stick with projects and undertakings, rather than allowing their natural restlessness to cause so many difficulties, not only for themselves but also for their families.

In The Home

The Archer needs space. It is vital. As a result, the Sagittarian home is likely to be as large as can be afforded and in an area where the surroundings give a degree of space – not for privacy, but for the freedom that a bit of extra room allows and the Sagittarian needs.

Sagittarians are likely to buy a property on impulse and are often attracted to older properties, but won't have a clue about any DIY, should this be necessary. They are also likely to want to move fairly regularly, as they are restless and get bored with routine.

Tidiness is not particularly important to the Archer, and the Sagittarian home will have that 'lived-in' look, and may often be downright untidy. It is important, however, that their homes are clean.

Books are likely to be an interest and so there will be a large number of bookshelves in their homes. They love to read and to learn and the majority of books in their collection will be reference books and encyclopedias. Their love of travel will mean that many travel books, both of places visited and those which they would like to visit, and objects picked up in foreign climes are also likely to feature largely in the household, as are many foreign language dictionaries and phrasebooks.

Sagittarians like parties, and their homes are often meeting places for large groups of people. They are good hosts but normally poor cooks.

Gardening is not likely to be an enduring pastime; the garden will look great when the mood takes and then be overlooked when the Archer's attention turns to other things.

Partnerships

Archers are one of the few signs that find it perfectly acceptable to have more than one partner at any one time. Affairs are likely for this sign, but they will be short-lived and any hint of permanence will see the whole thing called off. They need excitement in their lives, and anything routine is likely to them to seem boring and uninteresting.

As with Scorpions, Archers have a high sex-drive and a high energy-level and need fun in a relationship at all times. For this reason, they often prefer the wooing to the actual relationship. When the right partner comes along, however, they will be warm and gentle but unlikely to commit themselves easily to a long-term relationship which would stifle their freedom.

Likely to get on well with other fire signs and with air signs, Pisces, Cancer and Virgo subjects will be less likely choices of partners.

For the female Archer, a liaison with a Scorpio would be disastrous and Capricorn could also cause problems. A dalliance would be considered but anything more would be out of the question. Flirting appeals to the Archer; they think of it as a game, and they are fairly good at it, until their tendency towards tactlessness causes difficulties.

For the male Archer, Taureans would cause problems, and the best bet for both sexes would be Arians, although rivalries could be problematic.

Unlike most other star signs, two Sagittarians together could make a reasonable combination, as neither of them would notice the other's need for freedom or be jealous or resentful of them pursuing their own interests.

Sagittarians as Parents

Sagittarians get on well with children in the main, but put them with water or earth sign children and difficulties and misunderstandings will arise.

They don't take well to responsibilities and are likely to think long and hard about having a family and taking on more commitments. After all, having a long-term relationship is already a very large commitment for them.

Archer parents will encourage their offspring from an early age, and be very supportive, taking great delight in passing on the benefit of their wisdom and experience to their children and welcoming the opportunity to learn together. However, they are very unconventional people and are likely to encourage their children to learn all sorts of things away from the school curriculum. Education will always be important to the Sagittarian parent, whereas discipline might not.

Visits to other areas and other countries are more likely for the child of an Archer than most other signs, and the Sagittarian father in particular is likely to enjoy playing sports with the children. He would be delighted if his child suggested buying a horse, as riding is likely to appeal to him, even if he himself is unable to ride. Pets are also likely to be encouraged and the Sagittarian household often has several.

Similarly, the Archer mother will be very happy to play with the children, and long walks are likely to have great appeal. Many Sagittarian mothers need to have their own career or job outside the home, and the child of the Archer may have to learn self-sufficiency from an early age.

As the need for freedom is an important issue for Archers, they will instil this concept into their children and are very unlikely to be possessive parents; they will be particularly supportive when their children decide to leave home, as they themselves are likely to have left home at an early age.

Sagittarians as Siblings

Archer children are energetic, self-confident, independent, bright, alert and restless. They need to have a constant source of stimulation from a very early age to prevent them becoming bored and difficult. Discipline is needed when it comes to the Archer child.

Anything they find boring will be quickly discarded and whether in school or out, the Archer child will have a short concentration span. They also need to know the reasons behind everything, and 'Why?' is a question the Archer child will ask with an alarming frequency.

Their complete disregard for how they look will probably cause problems for them at school, and they will be untidy at home. A Libran sibling will find it very difficult to live with an Archer brother or sister.

They are also likely to be less concerned with time than any other sign, and anyone, sibling or adult, who suggests an outing must be prepared to wait for the Archer child. Once out, however, the sibling can expect lots of laughs and lots of fun. The Archer child will be in to everything and seem to have boundless energy and enthusiasm combined with a great sense of adventure.

Outbursts of temper will erupt on occasions and the siblings of an Archer must appreciate that nothing is really meant by the tirades of abuse which Archers tend to hurl, especially if their freedom is restricted or they feel they are being ordered about.

The Sagittarian sibling takes most things in his or her stride. They are most encouraging and supportive yet will probably want to leave the nest at the earliest opportunity. In adult life, however the Archer will keep in touch with his or her family, as security and roots somewhere are important.

Sagittarians as Friends

Sagittarians are very self-contained people and yet are also naturally friendly and have a large number of friends who will be invited to their house frequently. Their circle of friends, however, is likely to be ever-changing and long-standing friendships are rare. Warm, fun and good company, Sagittarians are always eager for any activity which seems different, especially if it involves sports.

If you have an Archer as a friend, you can be sure they will be totally honest with you, if not blunt, and you must be prepared for any tactless remarks they make. Chatty and communicative, never tell a Sagittarian a secret, because they are too truthful and indiscreet to keep it. Sagittarians have a good sense of humour and often their tactless remarks can be very amusing, unless of course it is at your expense.

Sagittarians at Work

Archers are optimists. Whatever career they have chosen, whether it is going well or not, they will be sure things will improve. Money is not the main focus in their work.

Anything involving travel will have huge appeal, as it will allow the Archers the freedom they need and the opportunity to indulge their sense of adventure. Similarly, anything of a pioneering nature will also have great appeal.

Having only a short concentration span, the Archer is useless at detailed work or anything routine, and working in an office from 9–5 will hold little interest, either in a junior or a senior post. If this becomes a necessity at any time in their career, they will happily off-load as much as they can on to willing shoulders. However, computing work may hold an interest. They are likely to be cheerful and helpful colleagues.

Living by their wits, and with a long list of people who can help them up the ladder of success, Archers tend to be very intuitive and taking risks holds no fear for them. Once established in a good position, they will still tend to flit from idea to idea, and take off at a moment's notice when the fancy takes them. Responsibilities do not sit well on their shoulders, and they can be very difficult to work for as a result. Not known for their tact and diplomacy, employees of the Archer have to be very thick-skinned.

The best jobs for the Archer are likely to be in travel, sales or public relations. Their love of other countries and the ease with which they learn other languages makes them good interpreters and their love of animals leads many of them to work with animals.

Their love of sports and natural sporting ability often means Archers are found working as sports coaches or professional sports-people, particularly golfers and horseriders. Their love of cars and fast transport could lead to more than a passing interest in these areas too.

Sagittarians and Health

Archers have huge amounts of energy, and anything which threatens this is likely to be feared, and this includes ill-health. Being ill means their freedom is restricted, and this they cannot take. Stress will be the outcome of any health worries, and consequently the problems could exacerbate. These times are probably the only occasions when Archers will experience stress, as their optimism and easy-going attitude to life will see them through in other difficult circumstances.

Most Archers will be fairly fit, although a few will be very lazy and need to be pushed to get trim. Sagittarians tend to like their food, and when depressed will indulge in bouts of comfort eating and drinking.

Hips and thighs tend to be a problem for Archers and if any weight is gained, it will immediately show here. At such times, they should try to decline offers of meals out, and watch portion sizes and fat content. Archers normally like fairly large amounts of food, especially dishes which are filling, stodgy and sweet. They also enjoy social drinking, and this can add to any weight problem they may have.

There is a tendency towards liver problems, sciatica and low-back pain and rheumatism, especially in old age. Their love of walking could help to keep them mobile when back problems strike and yoga could also help with maintaining flexibility.

Most Archers will take some form of exercise regularly, and anything which involves group activity will be of interest, although they are also happy to exercise on their own.

10

capricorn

Capricorn, 22 December – 20 January
*Capricorn – The tenth sign of the zodiac, and an earth
sign, ruled by Saturn. The sign for Capricorn represents
the original symbol of the goat with the fish's tail. It is said
that Capricorn was originally represented by the unicorn.*

Capricornians are traditional people, restrained and introverted, with
a practical and conventional nature. They exercise caution at all
times, are status-conscious, and totally reliable. They can also be
very ambitious.

Characteristics

Capricornians are stayers – people who keep going no matter what is thrown at them. They suffer with pessimism, and can worry about trivialities, but give them a goal to aim for and they will keep going until they get there.

Goats like to plan. They organise their days and can compartmentalise themselves to the extreme. They dislike delegation and often think nobody can do a job quite as well as they can.

They often seem aloof, but it is the reserved side of their nature which is being shown. They are, in fact, very warm and caring people, honest, sincere, responsible and faithful. They have a love of humanity, but are very often misunderstood, and their sense of humour is often mistaken for sarcasm.

Serious to a very large degree, Capricornians respect authority and react well to discipline. Give them a position of authority, and they command respect. Security matters to them, as does tradition. They are very patient people and also reliable and are conscious of what they perceive as duty.

Many people suggest that Capricornians are moody. A lot of this stems from the fact that they are essentially self-conscious, and hate to be pushed. They react in such instances by withdrawing and much prefer to be in the background. They have a dislike of 'labels' and anything which they consider unfair, especially when it relates to them.

They can be exceptionally stubborn, as befits an earth sign, and can tolerate the most unbearable situations and difficulties, when their responsible, self-contained nature seems to take over.

Secretive, fearing dislike and ridicule, Goats are often quite psychic.

Fashion

Traditional styles and traditional fabrics appeal to the conservative Capricornian. With an eye for a bargain, they often buy cheaply or from charity shops, as they don't see the point in spending unnecessarily on clothes. Like cars, which to them are simply a means of transport rather than anything else, clothes are things which merely serve a purpose. Greys, browns, and greens are likely to appeal to them and clothes must look well-cut and restrained; anything dark and understated will be chosen.

Money Matters

Money certainly does matter to the Goat. They can be very thrifty, and are often unfairly described as being mean. They know how to save, see no point in waste, and can be very ruthless when it comes to getting to the top in a job and earning extra money.

Capricornians often feel that they need to save their money for fear of a major misfortune. If a crisis should then occur, they are prepared and able to carry on without too much of a problem. They are quite happy to give to the less fortunate in society and will help friends out financially in times of trouble, but seldom forget this, and often expect to be eventually repaid in some way, despite their protestations to the contrary.

Spending money on the home is their one indulgence. They value their homes and consider that money spent there is an investment, as well as creating comfort and security.

Often considered to be misers and mean, Capricornians realise the purpose and value of money, and try to hang on to it. They will remember exactly how much money was loaned and will never forget the details of any financial transaction. They can often remember the sums involved many years afterwards, down to the last penny.

Improvements Needed

Capricornians need to learn to be less exacting, less pessimistic and less inhibited. They should also try to be less demanding of their partners.

Anything spontaneous is likely to be rejected, as they need to work to plans. They often do things because they think they are expected of them, rather than doing what they want to. As a result, resentment and frustration eventually set in.

Capricornians dislike taking chances and risks, and may often miss opportunities because of this. They should learn to exploit situations to the full and also realise that people in authority are not always right.

In The Home

Capricornians need their own homes to feel totally secure. Preferring something old and substantial to something new and skimped, they like a home that is economical to run, easy to maintain yet traditional. For this reason they often buy old houses which have been modernised.

They are likely to spend a lot of time in their homes and also spend a good deal of money on them. They like wood, and wooden kitchen fitments are likely to be top of the list of any improvements. They will happily work on their property themselves and are fairly practical when it comes to DIY.

Family pictures and family heirlooms will feature in the Goat's home. They will look after these inherited possessions and make sure they are handed down in the family tradition to the next generation. They especially like antiques and if they can afford to collect them, will indulge their interest shamelessly. If they do not have large sums of money to spare, they will look in bric-a-brac sales, junk shops or car boot sales for items which will appreciate in value. They will have good quality, highly-polished wooden furniture. Their homes will be tidy and clean, and even the garden will be well organised; anything disorganised or not working properly causes them a lot of stress. This does not mean that they can't be untidy; like most people, they can have spells, especially when depressed, of caring less about how they or the house look. When they do tidy up, however, they do so with a vengeance.

Most Capricornians enjoy gardening, especially as they get older and appreciate the relaxation it provides. However, they are not very keen on plants in the house; they will have a few odd ones which have been given as presents, but will never think of buying their own.

Capricornians like quiz shows and IQ tests, and anyone visiting their home must be prepared to sit through any such show on television. After that, their Capricornian host will be pleased to entertain them and is likely to be a good but traditional cook.

Partnerships

Their natural caution, tendency towards self-consciousness and reserved nature often mean that Capricornians have only a small circle of friends. Other people often see them as too serious and cold. Once they have broken the ice, however, Goats are good friends. They are very faithful and loving, yet often have difficulty showing their true emotions. They need a lot of support and praise and find it difficult to be open about their needs.

Unlikely to flirt, they need security and permanance in a relationship. One night stands have no appeal at all; they need to have someone they feel comfortable with and can trust. Once they have found that person, they can be fairly passionate and physically demanding partners.

Affairs hold little appeal either, unless there is an element of gain involved or they are truly unhappy in their existing relationship. Even then, they will think long and hard before embarking on an affair, as they are only too aware of emotional hurts themselves to do anything to hurt another. Any affair would have to be a secret to everyone apart from the people directly involved.

Likely to get on well with other earth signs, Capricornians can live with most other signs fairly happily, although Sagittarians may cause them difficulties.

In a relationship, Capricornians do well to avoid Geminians, Leos and Pisceans. Leos would be too bossy by far, and on the home front, Capricornians think of themselves as boss – which would not go down well with Leos, who tend to think likewise. Librans and Arians may also cause a problem for the Capricornian and rivalry may develop.

Capricornians as Parents

Capricornians like children, and once they feel they can relax, will play with them happily but still have strict rules and be quite disciplinarian, especially female Goats.

Unlikely to get on very well with Aquarian or Sagittarian children, Capricornian parents like organisation and will try to organise their children too, making sure they are well fed, well cared for, and also well behaved.

Capricornian fathers will work hard for their family, making sure that they want for nothing in the material sense. Education and learning will be encouraged and the Capricornian parent will make sure there are lots of reference books around the house to help with homework.

Capricornian parents will often indulge their children with presents and sweets; they need to feel loved, yet often find it difficult to express their own love for their children physically without the aid of presents.

Capricornian parents may expect their children to work for their pocket money by helping around the house or doing a paper round. They will also encourage their children to save and will expect a boy in particular to have proper training for his chosen profession. Goats worry naturally about their families, and want their children to be financially secure when they leave home.

Capricornian mothers will have set meal times, set bed times and agreed standards. The house will have a structured timetable and things must run smoothly. She may often seem to be unbending and rigid in outlook to her children, yet she will be loving and warm and try to create a strong family unit.

Any rift within the family will be felt deeply by the Capricornian parent, and at that time the Goat is likely to shed hidden tears of unhappiness.

Capricornians as Siblings

Capricornian children like to organise and may well include organising their siblings within their list of responsibilities. Any chance to take charge will be grabbed and they often seem a lot older than their years (possibly due to Saturn's influence). They will take school life very seriously; in fact it is fair to say that they take everything very seriously.

Interested in history, especially family history, the Capricornian child will have strong family values. He or she may often look to siblings for support, as they tend to lack self-confidence.

They are normally quiet children, and siblings who are a little too rowdy will be rebuffed. They respect their parents and are unlikely to get involved in anything which will lead to their parents' disapproval; they are far too sensible. As a result, they may be seen by their siblings as being 'spoil sports'. They often find it difficult to let themselves go and have fun, and play has to have a purpose, rather than just being play for its own sake. Often Goats only learn to play as they mature, and then realise what a lot they have missed.

A Capricornian sibling will always be there when needed, family duty and reliability being high on their list of priorities. Despite the fact that you may not get on with your Goat sibling, he or she will never let you down. If they say they will do something, they will, despite motivation not being one of their strong points.

Capricornians as Friends

Capricornians are selective when it comes to making friends, so if you have a Goat as a friend, you know you are valued! Likely to have a few close friends only, to a Capricorn a friend is a friend for life.

Capricornians are often regarded as anti-social, but in a friendship situation they are faithful and caring, and will do all they can to help, if asked. However, they will expect the same in return, if the tables are turned. Practical and supportive, the Goat friend will be there when you need them most, but will probably show you very little emotion; lots of sound advice and help will be in evidence, but feelings will be well hidden.

Capricornians tend to get on well with other earth signs, although Taureans' stubbornness will test their patience. They will also relate well to water signs. They would do well to cultivate the friendship of fire signs, who would bring them out of themselves and help them to have fun.

Capricornians at Work

Capricornians plan ahead from an early age and aim high. They have ambition and success is necessary for them to achieve the financial security they need.

Work and a steady career are important to the Capricornian. They dislike change and are likely to stay in a job for a long time if it suits their needs and their purpose. Depression is likely to set in should they feel undermined or unappreciated at work. They like to think they will receive regular promotions; they work hard, and expect to be noticed and rewarded.

Their standards of work are high, and they expect the same of others. They are disciplined and methodical and work well when set a challenge, working especially well to deadlines, but only if they know that the deadlines can be met. Totally reliable, if they take on a task, it will be seen through to the end. They tend to expect their colleagues, especially junior colleagues, to work in exactly the same way as them and at the same speed and find it difficult to understand that there can be several different ways of doing a job. When they ask for something to be done, they expect it to be done there and then and not to be put off until later.

They are naturally inclined to look towards a top job eventually, and once there will handle the responsibility well. A natural respect of authority leads them to expect this from their subordinates when they become boss, and they will be very unbending if this respect is not shown to them. They make very formal bosses and can be hard taskmasters, expecting their employees to toe the line. They will be very happy to lay on a large staff party at Christmas, but will wonder, however, why so few people are interested in going!

Possibly because they are shy, but maybe because they like to separate their working lives from their personal lives, they are unlikely to cultivate friendships at work.

Appropriate jobs for the Goat include management, teaching, building, farming, politics or administration. Male Goats may think about a career in engineering, architecture or surveying. Female Goats especially may think about a career helping the community.

Capricornians and Health

Depression, melancholia and anxiety are the main problems which beset the Goat. Learning to relax and learning to have fun are vitally important to their health and well-being. Problems with joints, especially knees, are likely for Capricorns, and in old age many suffer from rheumatism and arthritis. There is also a tendency towards skin problems and digestive difficulties, due mainly to over-acidity caused by nervous tension. Stress plays a huge part in the Goat's make-up. They tend to feel stressed in many circumstances, including when they are ill or when there are problems at work, especially if they feel they are not progressing up the ladder of success as quickly as they hoped. They cope well with success, but other changes are inherently disliked, especially if they do not form part of their master-plan. However, they often seem to thrive under pressure, and it isn't until they try to switch off at the end of it all that the stress will begin to show. If their security is threatened, or they are worried about being short of money, they will be especially stressed. Stress can often form a vicious circle of illness, although most Goats will fail to appreciate the need to relax a little.

Exercise will not normally fit into their scheme of things, unless there is a particular need or reason for it. Once undertaken, however, the regime will be organised and carried out methodically, but they are unlikely to want to join an exercise class, preferring to exercise on their own and in their own time.

Any diets will be strictly organised and a definite target set at an early stage. The best diet for them is probably counting calories or fat units, as they need this type of structured programme. They are normally pretty good at keeping their weight to an acceptable level, but personal difficulties will see them overeat and sink into depression. They can put on weight easily at such times, as Goats also tend to eat when bored.

Food is important to them, and they enjoy eating out when funds permit. They like traditional dishes and expect good-sized portions. They also like pasta and rice, and stodgy puddings. They would do well to use smaller dinner plates to avoid eating too much.

11

aquarius

Aquarius, 21 January – 19 February
Aquarius – The eleventh sign of the zodiac, and an air sign, ruled by both Uranus and Saturn. The sign for Aquarius represents rippling waves.

Aquarians are idealists, pioneers, leaders, and often years ahead of their contemporaries. They are humanitarians with strong communication skills and are generally out going.

Characteristics

Aquarians are restless people, forever searching for their ideal, and often lacking incentives. They care passionately about their fellow-man, and often this is at the expense of caring about themselves. They are very sociable people.

Placid, honest and truthful, these people thrive on debate but have difficulty coping with other people's opposing ideas.

Aquarians often have difficulty sharing emotions, and as a result experience problems with relationships. Essentially optimistic, they always hope things will improve, but find it difficult to discuss themselves and what motivates them.

Anything unusual or different will appeal to the Aquarian; they love anything original. Automatically drawn to group situations, they are good and loyal companions, and refreshingly unconventional. Anything petty or limiting will be disliked immediately, and situations or people who are unable to change will be rejected out of hand.

Fashion

Aquarians are not swayed by fashion trends. They wear what they like and what they think is most suitable for the particular occasion, irrespective of whether it is fashionable or not. They often favour well-fitting clothes.

Sometimes Aquarians dress quite dramatically to make a statement; at other times they will be quite subdued. Sometimes they choose colours which are bright and noticeable (like electric blue), sometimes something more refined and dark, or pale and subtle (like pale green).

In keeping with their futuristic ideas, many Aquarians wear things which look quite strange and are non-conformist.

Money Matters

While Aquarians realise the necessity for money, they are not drawn to strive long and hard to achieve material wealth, often looking on materialism as distasteful. Being rich is of no interest to these idealists. If they do become wealthy, they are likely to devote considerable time and money to charitable work, which appeals to their sense of honesty and humanitarianism.

Ideas and ideals are far more important to the Aquarian than money. Good at predicting trends, Aquarians sometimes make money by exploiting their ideas, but seldom enjoy the wealth that this can bring. The trappings of wealth hold little interest for them.

Improvements Needed

Aquarians need freedom and dislike any limitations. They can be very rebellious if they feel these basic essentials to life are challenged and become volatile and tactless. They care little what other people think of them and often do what they consider to be right, unaware of the impact this has on their families, friends or colleagues at work.

Aquarians should learn to work *with* their idealism, rather than let it work *against* them. They need to be more practical at times, and realise that the present matters as well as the future. They should also learn to be more open about their emotions especially with those around them.

In The Home

Aquarians regard home as the place you go to when you have nothing else to do. They are not interested in having a spotless or beautiful home but are nevertheless clean and tidy.

They usually have modern houses and their innovative ideas often lead them to have lots of plans for improvements. DIY holds no fears for them but they are not really practical people and often end up needing to call in professionals. Their colour schemes will be individual, if not bizarre!

Aquarians probably like moving home more than most signs. When the mood takes them and responsibilities permitting, they will happily move from house to house, bothering little about home comforts en route. They get bored easily, need freedom and are quixotic in nature. The only trappings of domesticity they care about tend to be kitchens or electrical gadgetry.

They are likely to have a mass of literature on their latest ideas or causes around the house and will probably have an interest in 'New Age' matters.

Concern with nature and the environment often leads Aquarians to being organic gardeners and conservationists. They enjoy originality in the garden and are likely to have some very exotic plants next to ordinary and traditional flowers.

Partnerships

Aquarians analyse people; they like to know what lurks under the surface. They are curious and often seem cold emotionally. Flirting appeals to them but more from an interest in the other person's mind rather than a physical attraction. Affairs hold little interest for the Aquarian.

Freedom will be important within any partnership, whether it be personal or business. Aquarians will not be restricted but in a happy relationship can be as supportive, loyal and faithful as anyone else. Marriage or a stable relationship will not be allowed to change their basic lifestyle.

There will always be something that they keep back to themselves in any relationship. They need something which is private and belongs to them only, and are unlikely to abandon themselves completely in a relationship. They don't like showing their feelings and may take a long time to settle into a relationship. Having found a partner, don't expect Aquarians to give up their large circle of friends. These are necessary to the Aquarian, and any threat to this need will be met with stubborn hostility.

Aquarians find problems dealing with emotions and anyone who is upset is likely to receive a cold shoulder from the Aquarian. This is quite unintentional but comes from the fact that they can't cope with overt signs of emotion. They can't cope with their own emotions, so how can other people expect them to cope with theirs!

Fairly good at keeping secrets, Aquarians make trustworthy partners. In a business relationship, they will be astute analysts and useful in predicting trends but not focused sufficiently to see a project through to completion. They can be very unpredictable. Rivalries are unlikely.

Cancerians, Virgoans and Pisceans may cause problems for the Aquarian, but nothing they can't handle. Arians, on the other hand, will produce a very unstable relationship, and Taureans will not be able to understand the Aquarian at all.

Two Aquarians together may be very successful, especially if they have similar ideals and don't argue.

Whatever the other star sign, a relationship with an Aquarian will be unpredictable, lively and unique.

Aquarians as Parents

Aquarian parents are very unorthodox yet encouraging. The responsibilities of parenthood do not lie well on their shoulders and often Aquarians will try to adopt the role of friend rather than parent to their offspring.

Virgoan, Capricornian and Piscean children may prove to be difficult for the Aquarian parent but most children will relish the freedom given to them by their Aquarian parents. Sensitive children may feel unwanted at times, especially in early childhood, but as the children grow up, the Aquarian parent will strive for a closer bond with them and be interested in discussing ideas with them. Should the child try to get the parent to change viewpoint, however, the conversation will become less friendly and open, as Aquarians rarely alter their opinions and resent their ideas being challenged, even by their children.

Aquarians are often difficult to understand, and the child of the Aquarian is likely to be confused as the parent changes direction quickly and without warning. Children may also find it difficult to cope with the lack of emotion shown by the Aquarian parent, especially when there is a crisis which needs parental support and response. While the Aquarian parent will help, they will show no obvious signs of emotion, even if the child is clearly distressed.

Aquarian fathers realise the need for security for their families, and resisting their natural instincts, will stick with a job or career they dislike, as long as it provides the necessary income to support the family.

Both Aquarian mothers and fathers can be disciplinarian one minute and totally lax the next. The children involved will often wonder what is happening. Mealtimes may also be haphazard where the Aquarian mother is concerned, especially if she is absorbed in a project which makes her lose all track of time.

Moving around appeals to the Aquarian, and there may be a temptation to uproot the family and move elsewhere with little thought being given to the children or their education.

Aquarian parents are nothing if not unconventional, and life with them is never dull.

Aquarians as Siblings

Aquarian children need their own space and value their own independence. They are generally creative and seem to prefer their own company to that of other children, who may often seem dull, slow and overemotional.

Their changeable nature will confuse most siblings, yet the Aquarian will often be unaware of the siblings' concern. Their inability to see the faults in others makes them think that others will react the same way towards them. Other people's worries tend to pale into insignificance in the overall scheme of things and the Aquarian child will be oblivious to everything going on around him or her.

Aquarian children have a dislike of authority and being told what to do, and a sibling who tries this is likely to be given the cold shoulder. Blunt and sometimes tactless, they upset others without meaning to. Once they have made a decision, they stick with it no matter what, even when it is obvious that the decision was wrong.

They are often seen as rebellious, but it is just that they have to do things their way and at their speed. They know what they want and will go all out to achieve it, with or without help from the family.

Aquarians are naturally intelligent and quick-minded and will either do well at school or become bored and disruptive. Being able to talk themselves out of trouble, they are often liked by teachers, who think of them as loveable rogues.

Aquarians as Friends

Easy-going, good company and sociable, Aquarians make good friends, just as long as you let them do what they want when they want to, and don't try to change them. They have a good sense of humour and can be witty companions.

Don't expect your Aquarian friend to tell you all their secrets, which will doubtless be many. They don't like emotional closeness in friendships and while they are happy to share your confidences, will be unlikely to discuss their own feelings with you.

Most Aquarians will have lots of friends and like group activities provided they are not overorganised and there are not too many rules to be followed. Anyone who shares common interests with the Aquarian will be encouraged, but still the Aquarian will need time alone to pursue the interest, and the friend must be prepared to understand this need. Freedom is vital to the Aquarian.

Likely to get on well with most people, Aquarians tend to find the happiest friendships with people from other air signs and also with fire signs, with the exception of Leos who are far too bossy for them.

Aquarians at Work

Aquarians prefer to keep job options open and will probably have several jobs, if not careers, during their working life.

Anything involving art or science is likely to appeal to the idealistic Aquarian, and computer work with its leanings towards the future would be a good choice of career.

Many Aquarians have an interest in astrology, and what may start as a hobby could well become a permanent job. They are good with people and anything involving working with people or the environment will give them the type of working situation they need. Other jobs for Aquarians to consider would be writing, science and psychology, as they have more than a passing interest in what makes other people 'tick'.

Injustice is something which the Aquarian hates. They will expect to be treated fairly and standards must be high. They will fight tooth and nail for the underdog and colleagues will appreciate their help at times when other signs may not have the courage to stand up to the management. Don't assume, however, that a close friendship will subsequently develop from such a situation; this is highly unlikely.

Routine jobs are likely to be rejected and while they will work hard on something they like, Aquarians will abandon anything they consider to be limiting or restrictive. They need to be given scope to work on new schemes and to experiment but they seldom have the stamina to see them through to completion. They will encourage the purchase of any new machinery or technology which will help in the work and Aquarian bosses are likely to be particularly popular with office machinery salesmen and computer companies!

Aquarians do not look for top management positions or jobs with status and responsibilities. They need to be able to change course when it suits them and having employees to consider would make their lives difficult. They can be selfish when they choose and their tendency to be oblivious to things going on around them can make them seem aloof and cold. However, they often do rise to the top simply because they have different ideas and a fresh approach.

Aquarians and Health

Problems with ankles, legs and circulation are the main health difficulties which the Aquarian is likely to encounter. At times of stress, such as pregnancy or when family difficulties occur, or if anyone tries to place too many restrictions on them, many Aquarians will develop swollen ankles or varicose veins.

Quite highly strung, despite their carefree appearance, Aquarians often suffer with their nerves and will probably be interested in trying complementary medicines and therapies.

Some Aquarians have problems with their weight all their lives, some have none at all. They enjoy food, but it is not of great importance to them. Should a diet be necessary, anything different will appeal and should allow for at least one meal out a month (which will be to a different place each time!). A set diet or rigid regime will have no attraction whatsoever for Aquarians and they are highly unlikely to even think about joining a slimming club, as they would dislike the rules and regulations involved.

Exercise is not likely to play a major part in the Aquarian's lifestyle. Walking or golf would probably be the only activities they would seriously consider. Surprisingly, most Aquarians dislike watersports and so swimming, despite its calorie-burning potential, is unlikely to be an option.

Aquarians like the widest range of foods, and will come up with the strangest combinations – having a meal with an Aquarian is usually very interesting!

12

pisces

Pisces, 20 February – 20 March
Pisces, the twelfth and final sign of the zodiac, and a water sign, ruled by Neptune. The sign for Pisces represents two fish joined together.

Pisceans are very sensitive people, emotional and intuitive with a natural empathy, receptiveness and passivity. They are often very mediumistic or psychic.

Characteristics

Pisceans are very lovable people. They have a sensitivity towards all groups and classes of people and are compassionate and caring.

Any problems brought to their door will be dealt with sympathetically and it is not unknown for them to weep at the suffering of others. To some this is an indication that they are too sensitive and over emotional but to others it is just a confirmation of the caring nature of these people.

There is a tendency with Pisceans to sacrifice themselves to the whims and desires of other people. In an emotional relationship, Pisceans are likely to be unconditional in their love and rather naive; they hate to think that they have caused hurt to anyone or anything.

Often artistic or musical, Pisceans are sometimes regarded as dreamers. They love to escape into a book or film; readily drifting into the plot and losing themselves easily, they can often find it difficult to distinguish between fantasy and reality. Similarly, they are very receptive to and affected by the environment in which they may find themselves. They are sensitive to atmospheres and to the feelings of others, and are easily swayed by other people to change their viewpoint.

Pisceans are often changeable and indecisive. Because they have no firm viewpoint of their own, they are willing to listen to anyone else's, something which if pointed out to them, they will deny vigorously. They seldom see themselves in their true light.

Gullible and easily taken in, Pisceans often confide in the wrong people. They need to have an emotional closeness with another person but often become totally dependent and lose their own identity. At such times, they resort to humour to pull them through.

Fashion

Individual in dress, Pisceans usually go for subtle styles and colours, and soft greens, mauves and greys are likely to attract them. Anything romantic will appeal to the female Fish; the male Fish is happy as long as he is comfortable.

Money Matters

Pisceans are not normally interested in material things. Realising its necessity (as with Aquarians), Fish are not really bothered about money. Don't assume from this that they do not want to make money and have a good and solid career, because this is not so. They like to have nice things and value security in their lives, but are happy either way. If they should lose money or do not earn much, they won't mind. As long as they have their ideals and dreams, they are happy. Saving for the future does not enter their thoughts at all. Pisceans are not good at budgeting, and as a result are often overspent; they are too extravagant and spend without thinking of the consequences.

Improvements Needed

Pisceans love to complain and often take on other people's problems as well as their own and then bemoan the burden they carry.

Too sensitive, too caring, too dependent on others and too emotional, they need to learn to differentiate between their own ideas and those of others and between what they would ideally like and dream about and what really is possible.

Not good at problem solving, Pisceans often seem scatty, incomprehensible and impractical. They should try to curb their tendency towards escapism and face up to realities. They should listen to their own intution when making decisions and not be swayed by others.

In The Home

The Piscean home is an important place as it provides a retreat from the outside world. Pisceans will live anywhere, as long as it provides some form of seclusion and is accessible. They prefer a quiet, private environment to anything too noisy, and yet often end up living in places they dislike because of pressure from those around them.

Pisceans are not known for their tidiness. They seem to live in permanent turmoil, and their houses reflect this. Cleaning is something which can be overlooked, but nevertheless the Piscean home will be a comfortable place, although it will have a 'well-used' look and feel.

DIY will be attempted, gardens will be romantic, but the whole image will be of disorganization. A perfect house and garden are not likely with the Fish in charge. Objects will be scattered all over the place and nothing will be co-ordinated. However, female Fish may have an interest in flowers or flower arranging and the home is likely to look artistic, if nothing else.

One thing which will certainly feature in the Piscean home is music. If the Piscean is musical, an instrument will feature; if not, there will be records, CDs, tapes and radios – most Pisceans will indulge their love of music daily and throughout the house.

Partnerships

Pisceans can be difficult to live with and in turn find others difficult to live with. They fall in love easily and often with the wrong people. Not ones to admit this, however, they will make the most of the situation and try to be as loving and caring as they possibly can. They don't like facing up to facts.

There are times when the Piscean will seem overemotional and times when, due to tension either within the home or at work, they are downright awkward. However, they will fail to realise what they are like and life for those around them will prove difficult.

Sharing is important to the Piscean. Romance is also very important and Pisceans tend to lose themselves in the idealism of the situation. They enjoy flirting, both inside and outside a relationship. Male Fish are very likely to shower the object of their affection with flowers, chocolates and gifts, often unable to see any flaws in the character of their partner. They can, however, become very jealous if they think their partner is showing attentions elsewhere, even if this is not so. A partner who flirts will cause problems for the sensitive Fish, who is unable to see the problems that their own, similar behaviour patterns cause.

Affairs are unlikely, although not impossible. The only time this may be considered is on a 'one night stand' basis, and this will be rare.

In a business partnership, Pisceans are happy to work alongside anyone, and rivalries are very unlikely indeed.

In most cases, Pisceans react well with other water signs, and also with Taureans and Capricornians. Geminians and Sagittarians are likely to be hard to get on with.

Female Fish may find Aquarians difficult to relate to, and male Fish will find Arians and Cancerians totally impossible.

Two Fish together make a good combination, as they will both be able to cope with their disorganised lifestyles without even noticing a problem!

Pisceans as Parents

Piscean parents are very supportive and encouraging towards their offspring. Their problems lie in exerting discipline and their children tend to exploit their laxness.

Taureans, Arians and Sagittarian children are likely to be problems for the Fish, but most other children will respond well to Piscean parents.

Pisceans seem to retain the ability to 'see as a child', and as such are often good teachers to their children. Willing to spend a lot of time talking and listening, Pisceans often spend so much time with their families that other things go completely by the board.

Not renowned for their time-keeping, Pisceans dislike regimentation, and their children will be brought up to be free-thinking and independent.

Pisceans cannot cope well with restrictions and they find it difficult to say 'No'. A skilful child can utilise this to his or her own advantage.

Piscean mothers may well be so disorganised that they forget meal times, shopping or packed-lunches. However, she will be full of emotional encouragement, and will be willing to give up anything to help her children, often arranging outings for them which means she has to forego something she had previously arranged for herself.

Often forgetting that other people are not quite like them, Pisceans can find parenthood difficult, especially with an academic or logical child who has only limited imagination.

Loving and imaginative, Piscean parents are brilliant at bedtime stories, but may forget what time bedtime is supposed to be!

Piscean fathers who have difficult jobs are likely to want to unwind in peace and solitude at the end of the day and children who encroach on this time are likely to be rebuffed. Piscean parents often find having a family somewhat disillusioning.

Pisceans as Siblings

Pisces children are generally well behaved, but need to learn to deal with one thing at a time and to concentrate better. They seem to forget things as soon as they have been told and this includes rules and regulations.

As children, Pisceans often have a fear of the dark and need help to get to sleep. Trouble can result from an older sibling putting fears into the mind of the young Fish – they have a vivid imagination which is easily stirred.

They are normally quiet, artistic children and can be easily upset if anyone bullies them or if they think they are being ignored.

They cry easily and the sibling of the Fish is likely to see this behaviour at first hand quite frequently. A tidy sibling who shares a room with a Fish is likely to find lots of tears when the Fish is told to tidy up.

Imaginative and caring, the Fish child is likely to invent all sorts of games and fantasies, and writing short stories is likely to appeal greatly, once the child is old enough. Younger siblings are likely to have these stories 'tried out' on them, and would be well advised not to criticise!

Piscean children are not discriminating about whom they have as friends and as a result can be easily hurt and bullied. Strong, older siblings (Leos for example) would do well to look after their young Fish. They are easily led and make terrible mistakes, especially in early maturity.

Piscean children generally like swimming and water sports, often in preference to homework, and a sibling who shares this interest is likely to find a very happy Fish. However, the Fish will always need a lot of encouragement and support, and while they are happy to share their time and toys with others, selfish siblings are likely to cause them a lot of heartache.

Pisceans as Friends

Caring, warm, sympathetic, helpful – all these things combined make a Piscean friend. They will do anything they can to help their friends and need people around them to function effectively.

Never ever tell your Piscean friend a secret, because they cannot keep confidences. They may have quite a few of their own, but because they find it difficult to share their emotions, may not be able to talk about their own worries.

Pisceans are artistic and anyone who shares their interests is likely to be a good friend. They like beauty and value it highly and therefore get on well with other water signs and also with

Librans and Aquarians. They tend to dislike shopping and crowds, and in this respect have a lot in common with Librans. However, Librans would hate their untidiness.

Pisceans at Work

Their natural, artistic leanings tend to make Pisceans very good artists, writers, musicians, photographers, dancers and actors. Anything too logical, noisy, routine or analytical will be a poor choice of career; they will be unable to cope with the restrictions and discipline involved.

Nursing would be a good profession to consider, because Pisceans like looking after other people and are naturally altru-istic. However, they would probably prefer community nursing to working in a large hospital with its rules and regulations.

Not particularly concerned about earning a lot of money the importance lies in doing what they feel happy with, and as long as they follow their heart in such matters, it is not uncommon for them to achieve great success. If they are happy in a job, they will devote time and energy to it and do their very best at all times, not for the chance of being rewarded or promoted but because they enjoy it. Their love of the sea can lead many Fish to jobs involving travel, whether this be in the services or in the tourist or travel industry.

Pisceans are popular workmates. They are seldom interested in making a mark or in rivalries and will happily get on with their job, probably unaware of anybody else, unless of course an atmos-phere or argument develops, when the Fish will become very tense. Their desks are likely to be messy and nobody else will be able to find anything, but they are supportive to their colleagues, and aren't worried about climbing to the top of the ladder.

If they do reach the top of their profession, it is likely to be by chance rather than by design. As bosses, they rely heavily on their staff helping them with organisational matters. They can come up with ideas, but need help with the groundwork and a lot of support.

Loyal to their staff, and expecting the same in return, the Piscean boss will make sure that pay rises are regular and as good as possible and that people are fairly rewarded for hard work. Difficulties lie in their tendency to change their minds and they need continued help and support to see projects through.

Pisceans and Health

Stress, tension and nervous problems take their toll on the Fish and when things are not going too well, they can take to drink as a way out.

Anything involving change will be a cause of stress for the Piscean. Moving home or having a family are all reasons for stress. Anything too regimented or unbending will also cause stress for the Fish. They need to be in a happy environment and often cope with pressure by going off into their own dreamworld, and shutting out reality.

Although they can eat quite a lot on occasions, Pisceans tend to drink more than they eat. They like lemony things, natural foods and fruit juices. They often have a problem with salt, and if they want to cut down on anything, they should definitely restrict their salt-intake.

They are good cooks and quite creative in the kitchen. They are likely to devise their own recipes and are excellent hosts. They can develop weight problems because they are genuinely unaware of how much they are eating. Fluid retention can be a problem for them and female Fish may have a monthly problem with this. They can diet easily and stick to a diet well but need to have supportive friends to keep them on the straight and narrow.

Swimming would be good exercise to combine with any diet. Fish are not naturally competitive but exercise well when they decide they must. Dancing is something which could help with weight reduction and anything with music will be enjoyed, although whatever exercise they decide upon must be unstructured and not routine.

Fish should be careful with their feet and especially their toes, as they tend to have problems with bunions, corns, chilblains etc.

13

using the star signs

We have now covered all the basic star sign information necessary to understand both ourselves and those around us a little better.

You should have been able to identify various characteristics of family and friends, and maybe have been able to see faults in yourself which you can rectify.

Learning should not stop once a subject has been mastered; the trick comes in utilising the knowledge gained. Hopefully, you will have realised both your strengths and weaknesses and now be able to work on neutralising some of the negativities in your character.

Looking for a Job?

If you have a job at the moment, are you really happy in it? Does it satisfy any creative ambitions or interests, or are you doing it merely for the monetary reward? Take another look at the *At work* section for your own sign and see what is listed there. Remember, if you were born within the three or five days of the end of a sign or during the three or five days at the start of a sign, look at the other star sign to see what information is given there.

There are times in everybody's lives, not just for mid-life Sagittarians, when you take stock of things and decide upon a change of job. The difficulty usually lies in being true to yourself and your family and being aware of the financial implications of change. Any help that astrology can give must surely be welcome.

Thinking along the lines of applying for a new job, make sure you take into account all your strengths. Look at the characteristics for your sign and list all the relevant qualities which apply to the job in question and don't merely base your CV on the requirements listed in the advertisement for the job.

Looking for Love?

If you are looking for a partner, bear in mind the advice on star sign compatibilities. For your help and information, there is a simple chart at the end of this chapter identifying the best options and those which are least likely to provide happiness. Should your prospective partner (or indeed your current partner) not rate highly in this chart, don't despair and end the relationship. Natal charts for you both could indicate reasons why what is seen as a possibly difficult relationship in our chart could in reality work well. Just bear in mind the generalities of the union. Look at the strengths and weaknesses of the person. Compare these to your own. Identify for yourself where potential problems could occur, and make every effort to work towards alleviating these, if possible before they become serious.

Problems in the Family?

If you are a sensitive Piscean and have a boisterous Arian as a brother or sister, you may be having problems. Look to see what common ground you can share. Likewise, if you are a Capricornian parent and are having a lot of difficulties with your child, look to see why. If the child is a Sagittarian, the answer is obvious. If the child, however, is a Taurean, maybe there are things which need addressing, as the relationship should run smoothly. Should your child be having difficulties at school, look to see what information we have on the child, and bear in mind the need for support and encouragement or the need the child might have to be left alone.

Need to Diet?

At some stage, most of us need to diet, and indeed, some of us seem to be on a permanent diet. If it is not working, look to see what information we have in the *Health* section for your sign. Identifying the type of diet best suited to your star sign, you should be able to lose weight more effectively. You will also see what forms of exercise you are best suited for, and maybe identify something that you have not previously considered.

Buying a Present?

Are you about to buy a present for a Taurean? Take a look at the information we have on the Bull. You will see that Taureans like gardening and are normally good with plants. You will also see that they are home-loving people. Try to base your choice of present on these facts, and you will be sure not to go far wrong. Buying for a Capricornian? Look for either something in wood or something traditional. Many Capricornian men have large collections of things already. Try to buy something that will fit in with these facts.

Astrology can help with all these sorts of problems. It is not merely a question of whether you are likely to have a good day or not. It helps to identify how we relate to other people and indeed, how we relate to ourselves.

Before we finish this book, let's have a few practice questions. From these, you should be able to guess which star sign I belong to!

Practice

• Terry is a Virgoan. He is 17 and studying at school. He would like some help on careers to which he might be suited. Bearing in mind this is the only information we have on Terry, what would be your advice?

• Gloria is a Leo. Her mother is a Taurean. They seem to be having problems and Gloria wants to leave home. She is 22 and has a good job and is earning good money. Gloria is beginning to feel she doesn't understand her mother's needs at all. What general advice and/or forecasts could you give, based on characteristics, on:

how Gloria will cope when moving into her own place and paying the bills?

her mother's feelings if and when Gloria moves out? There is no need to be too specific here, and if the situation ever presents itself and you are asked for this sort of advice, be very careful both in what you say and how you say it.

• Mary is an Aquarian. Her boyfriend is a Libran. Are they likely to get on well? They are considering marriage.

- Susan is a Libran. She is thinking of asking her friend Joan to share a flat with her. Joan is a Piscean. What immediately springs to mind about this combination when it comes to sharing a property. Think in terms of personal standards rather than anything else.

Having read this book, and bearing in mind what we have discussed in this chapter, maybe you can now see how astrology can help us all in our lives.

If you are interested in learning more about astrology, there are several very good books around, and some of them are listed at the end of this text. A very good book to start with would be Jeff Mayo's *Teach Yourself Astrology*.

Astrology is both fascinating and helpful; let it help you!

General compatibilities

	Aries	Taurus	Gemini	Cancer	Leo	Virgo	Libra	Scorpio	Sagittarius	Capricorn	Aquarius	Pisces
ARIES	3	1	3	6	1*	3	1	1*	2	2	3	6
TAURUS	2	2	5	3	1*	2	1	2	6	1	1	2
GEMINI	3	4	4	6	2	5	1*	3	3	5	4	6
CANCER	5	2	6	1*	5	3	5	6	4	2	5	6
LEO	3	1	1*	1	5	5	2	3	2	5	4	5
VIRGO	6	2	1	4	4	5	4	1	3	2	5	1*
LIBRA	4	1	1	4	2	5	5	3	3	6	1*	2*
SCORPIO	2*	3	5	1	2	2	5	3	4	2	4	1*
SAGITTARIUS	1*	4	3	5	2	2	2	6	2	6	5	5
CAPRICORN	3	3	5	1	5	4	5*	1	6	1	1*	1
AQUARIUS	2	4	4	5	2	5	1*	4	3	4	1	5
PISCES	4	1	3	2	2	3	1	2	5	1	5	1*

Key to the codes

1* = The best
1 = Very good/passionate
2 = Good
3 = Maybe

4 = Will need working on
5 = No
6 = Disastrous

further reading

Birbeck, Lyn, *Sun, Moon and Planet Signs*, Bloomsbury Press, England, 1992

Geddes, Sheila, *Astrology and Health*, Aquarian Press, Wellingborough, 1981

Harding, Michael & Harvey, Charles, *Working with Astrology*, Penguin/Arkana, 1991

Lewi, Grant, *Astrology for the Millions*, Llewellyn/Foulsham, 1992

McEvers, Joan, *Financial Astrology for the 1990s*, Llewellyn/Foulsham, 1991

Merlin, Katharine, *Character and Fate*, Penguin/Arkana, 1991

Parker, Derek & Julia, *The Compleat Astrologer*, Mitchell Beazley, 1979

Seymour, Percy, *Astrology – The Evidence of Science*, Penguin/Arkana, 1991

Stone, Pauline, *Relationships, Astrology and Karma*, Aquarian Press, Wellingborough, 1992

Tompkins, Sue, *Aspects of Astrology*, Element Books, England, 1991

Zolar, *Zolar's Starmates*, Simon and Schuster, London, Sydney, New York, Tokyo, Toronto, 1992